ISBN 978-1-333-88593-9
PIBN 10741467

This book is a reproduction of an important historical work. Forgotten Books uses state-of-the-art technology to digitally reconstruct the work, preserving the original format whilst repairing imperfections present in the aged copy. In rare cases, an imperfection in the original, such as a blemish or missing page, may be replicated in our edition. We do, however, repair the vast majority of imperfections successfully; any imperfections that remain are intentionally left to preserve the state of such historical works.

1 MONTH OF
FREE
READING

at
www.ForgottenBooks.com

By purchasing this book you are eligible for one month membership to ForgottenBooks.com, giving you unlimited access to our entire collection of over 700,000 titles via our web site and mobile apps.

To claim your free month visit:
www.forgottenbooks.com/free741467

English
Français
Deutsche
Italiano
Español
Português

www.forgottenbooks.com

Mythology Photography **Fiction**
Fishing Christianity **Art** Cooking
Essays Buddhism Freemasonry
Medicine **Biology** Music **Ancient
Egypt** Evolution Carpentry Physics
Dance Geology **Mathematics** Fitness
Shakespeare **Folklore** Yoga Marketing
Confidence Immortality Biographies
Poetry **Psychology** Witchcraft
Electronics Chemistry History **Law**
Accounting **Philosophy** Anthropology
Alchemy Drama Quantum Mechanics
Atheism Sexual Health **Ancient History**
Entrepreneurship Languages Sport
Paleontology Needlework Islam
Metaphysics Investment Archaeology
Parenting Statistics Criminology
Motivational

133388i

TO THE REVEREND

CHARLES MATTHEW EDWARD-COLLINS, CLERK, M.A.,

OF TREWARDALE,

IN THE COUNTY OF CORNWALL,

AS AN ACKNOWLEDGEMENT OF A LONG AND VALUED FRIENDSHIP,

AND IN GRATEFUL RECOGNITION OF THE INTEREST

HE HAS TAKEN IN THE "HISTORY OF THE DEANERY OF TRIGG MINOR" FROM ITS COMMENCEMENT,

AS WELL AS OF THE VALUABLE ASSISTANCE

HE HAS KINDLY RENDERED IN ITS COMPILATION,

THIS VOLUME IS AFFECTIONATELY

DEDICATED

BY THE AUTHOR.

Plate II

VIEW OF ST. TEATH CHURCH.

from a Photograph.

J. Ferguson, Lith.

Maclure & Macdonald, Lith.rs to the Queen, London.

PARISH OF ST. TEATH.

The parish of St. Teath derives its name from the dedication of the Church, whose Patron Saint is St. Thetha. It contains by admeasurement 5839 acres, and is bounded on the northwest by the sea; on the north by the parishes Tintagel and Lanteglos; on the east by Minster, Lanteglos, Michaelstow, and St. Tudy, and on the northeast by St. Kew and St. Endellion. The following particular perambulation, made in 1613, is preserved in the Bishop's Registry at Exeter.

Cornwall.〕 A RECORD of. the circuit of the Boundes and Lymites of the pish of St. Teath
St. Teath │ vewed and seene by the Minister and pishioners there Annoque domini 1613.
Boundes 〉   Boundes beginninge at nuell Mill and goinge vp along by y᷎ hedge vpright next
Ann° D'ni │ adioyninge till it come to John Sloggat's meadow, soe turning, y᷎ new hedge y᷎ bound
1613. 〕 south and leadinge vpright from y᷎ end of y᷎ hedge to y᷎ Longe Stone in John Sloggat's ground ptinge betweene Lanteglos & St. Teath; and from the Longe Stone aforesaid runninge vpright to y᷎ cross in the Lane and soe ·boundinge along by y᷎ highwaie by y᷎ Lane till it come to the head of Castlegow ground. All the ground next adioyninge w᷎ Trevighen ground and goinge vp along to y᷎ head of Castlegow ground as on y᷎ other side being bounded w᷎ y᷎ bonds bet. bounds in St. Teath. The Corn & Sheer of all the said groundes the tithe cometh vnto St. Teath, and y᷎ rest of all other small tithes att Lanteglosse: And soe boundinge alonge northward by Castlegow hedge till it come to Trewen ground ptinge betweene Lanteglosse & St. Teath aforesaid. Soe boundinge along northward by y᷎ hedge till it come to the corner of Dillinuth Downe ioyninge w᷎ Dellie, soe boundinge alonge the hedge eastward against Hendra & Dellie ptinge betweene Lanteglosse and St. Teath aforesaid and leadinge alonge by y᷎ hedge from Hendra northwards till it come to delie yeat in y᷎ lane, and from thence y᷎ hedge right northward till it come to little Trethen, and boundinge alonge northward to great Trethen ground; then boundinge alonge y᷎ hedge till it come to certaine closes, called the Roses, in Trethen: and soe boundinge alonge eastward by the hedge till it come to a lyttle water boundinge betweene Lantegloss on the one side, Minster on y᷎ other, & St. Teath on the other, and soe boundinge alonge y᷎ hedge northward againe till it come to Pendevie well ptinge betweene Minster & St. Teath aforesaid, leadinge vp alonge y᷎ hedge till it come to the cross lane to Bruer's yeat ptinge betweene Minster, Lanteglosse, & St. Teath: and turninge Westward alonge y᷎ highwaie y᷎ hedge y᷎ bound till it come to Medders ground: forsakinge y᷎ highwaie goinge Westward betweene Penpethie and Medders ground, ptinge betweene Lanteglosse and

N

St. Teath aforesaied, and soe boundinge alonge y⁰ hedge to Nedders Corner ptinge betweene Lanteglosse, Tintagell, & St. Teath, and soe leading from Nedders Corner alonge y⁰ hedge till it come to y⁰ highwaie ptinge between Tintagel and St. Teath afores⁴, leadinge along y⁰ waie westward y⁰ hedge y⁰ bound till it come to y⁰ downe; and soe boundinge alonge y⁰ downe till it come to a lyttle white stone in y⁰ downe ptinge betweene Tintagel & St. Teath; then boundinge from y⁰ white stone alonge by an olde bound till it come to Corcuddle corner, beinge the head bound, & soe turninge northwest by an olde bound till it come to Trevela Corner ptinge betweene Tintagel and St. Teath, and soe leadinge to Trevela yeat, and from thence alonge by y⁰ hedge northwest betweene Trevela & Treburget, and soe the water runninge downe to y⁰ sea beinge y⁰ bound betweene Tintagell & St. Teath afores⁴. And by the Clifte westward boundinge along by y⁰ sea till it come to Eudellion betweene Hendra of St. Teath and Scrub Hendra of Endellion; from thence boundinge by a hedge southeast till it come to y⁰ highwaie next adioyninge wᵗʰ Treora ground, and from thence southeast by y⁰ hedge till it com to a corner of a close called y⁰ Shutthell pke ptinge betweene St. Teath & Endellion & St. Kew: and soe leadinge alonge southeast till it com to y⁰ highwaie, and y⁰ highwaie turning northeast by y⁰ hedge till it come to Hendra Cross, beinge y⁰ bound ptinge betweene St. Kew & St. Teath afores⁴, and from Hendra Cross over y⁰ downe by an olde bound leading to a lane betweene Chenie Downe & Trewicket, ptinge betweene St. Kew and St. Teath; and from thence south by a new hedge betweene Chenie Downe & Trewicket y⁰ higher, thence leadinge by y⁰ hedge southeast betweene Trewicket aforesaid & Trekee vnto a water betweene ffentengooge & Trekee aforesayd, ptinge betweene St. Kew & St. Teath aforesayed. ffrom thence leadinge along the lane, beinge y⁰ highwaie, till it come to Pengennoe yeate. And from thence y⁰ hedge leadinge betweene Treburgate & Pengenna till it com to a place called ffoxehoole beinge the bound betweene St. Kew and St. Teath, and from thence to a meadow northward ioyning wᵗʰ y⁰ river wᶜʰ ioynes wᵗʰ Polroade in St. Tiddye, thence leadinge to y⁰ River beinge y⁰ bound to Terrenicke bridge, ptinge betweene St. Tiddye & St. Teath aforesaid, and so bounding alonge y⁰ river till it come to Knights Mill bridge, beinge y⁰ bound ptinge betweene Michelstow, Lanteglos & St. Teath aforesayd, and soe boundinge vp alonge y⁰ Riuer till it come to Nuell Mill ptinge betweene Lanteglosse & St. Teath aforesayed, beinge the verye place where y⁰ boundes began.

Wee fynde that the overside of the river against Lanuagou ground that there is one little [illegible] of moore grounde wᶜʰ belongs vnto Tintagel aforesaid contayning by estimation [illegible] yeards, or neare thereabouts.

Nycholas Edward,
Thomas Nichole, } *Churchwardens.*

Though there are 200 acres of common in the parish, the land, generally, is fertile, chiefly arable. The principal landowners are Lord Robartes, Honble. G. M. Fortescue, S. M. Grylls, and Nicholas Male, Esquires.

The chief villages are the Church Town, Medrose, Pengelly and Treligga.

Besides the cultivation of the soil, in which the inhabitants are chiefly occupied, about 300 men are employed in the famous Delabole slate quarry, and nearly 200 persons, men, women, and children, in Treburget Mine; though neither of these is worked to the same extent as formerly. Agricultural laborers receive, as elsewhere in the neighbouring parishes, about 12s. a week. At the quarry artificers earn about 20s. a week, and quarrymen about 14s. At the mine earnings range from 15s. to 25s. a week.

There are two fairs held annually at the Church Town, one on the 23rd February, and the other on the 6th of June.

The following table will show the population, and the number of houses inhabited, uninhabited, and building, at the several decennia when the census was taken in the present century.

				1801	1811	1821	1831	1841	1851	1861	1871
Population	..	..	..	911	857	990	1260	1719	2204	1980[1]	2245
Houses	Inhabited	..	..	150	134	151	251	339	429	405	468
	Uninhabited	..	..	8	2	5	9	31	61	46	22
	Building	..	..	..	..	2	7	2	1	1	..

ASSESSMENTS, &c.

	£	s.	d.
Annual Value of Real Property Assessed upon the parish in 1815 ...	5,041	0	0
Rated Value from County Rate, 1866	6,816	0	0
Gross Estimated Rental, 1866	8,091	0	0
Rateable Value in 1866 ...	7,194	0	0
Gross Estimated Rental in 1875 ...	9,116	0	0
Rateable Value in 1875 ...	8,289	0	0
Parochial Assessments, 1874:—			
Poors' Rate ...	641	0	0
Sanitary Rate ...	15	0	0
Highway Rate ...	396	0	0
Police Rate ...	91	13	4
County Rate ...	75	0	0
Land Tax:—			
Redeemed ...	78	14	1½
Payable	82	13	10½
Inhabited House Duty Assessed upon the Annual Value of ...	115	0	0
Property and Income Tax Assessed upon Schedule A ...	7,426	0	0
„ „ „ B ...	6,151	0	0
„ „ „ D ...	Not known.		
„ „ „ E ...	Not known.		

[1] The decrease is attributed to the closing of slate quarries and mines.

N²

GEOLOGY.

This parish rests upon the Devonian series of rocks, and into which protrudes for about half a mile the Elvan dyke, already described,[1] and a greenstone vein running parallel with it, on the east side, for a somewhat greater distance.   There is also another small vein of greenstone running parallel with the river boundary on the east of the parish, and reaching from Treharrick to near Knight's Mill.   The argillaceous slates of this parish underlie the grauwack slates and grits of Boscastle and Tintagel, which are beneath the carbonaceous series of North Devon.   In several places, particularly at the celebrated Delabole Quarries, these slates are of a sufficiently fine grain to be worked as roofing slates, and are superior to any in the district.   They are even said by Bishop Watson in his "Chemistry" to be the very best in England.   Interspersed with these are found schistose beds, resembling green-stone, which, in some places, so graduate into the slate that the change becomes imperceptible, forming a kind of porphyry.   These beds appear to consist of finely comminuted greenstone permitted to settle in water in which calcareous matter was occasionally present.   Dr. Boase has observed that the principal mineral substance has a character between hornblend and chlorite.   Throughout the Delabole Quarries there are insular patches of the same rock which have not regular foliation, but which break into coarse thick fragments, with a conchoidal fracture.   In some places they resemble roofing slate, but in others they contain a considerable portion of a dark green foliated hornblend, similar to that occurring in conjunction with calcareous spar in the rock at Grylls, before described,[2] and a mineral in the form of white streaks of carbonate of lime.   This circumstance shews that the slate of Delabole forms part of the series of rocks to which the calcareous rocks of Grylls belong.   The whole may be regarded as one system, the two kinds of trappean rock having, probably, been erupted, one in the state of igneous fusion and the other in that of ash, during the time that the mud now forming slates was deposited.

At Treburget is a mine of lead, silver, and copper, which has been worked with great advantage, and is still in operation, but it is understood not to be so rich as formerly.   The lodes run north-east and south-west, varying from two feet to five feet in thickness.   The matrix of the ores consists of angular pieces of slate like fragments cemented by quartz, in which galena, blende, iron pyrites, and spathose iron occur.[4]

---

[1] Hist. of Trigg, Vol. ii., p. 79, and Vol. iii, p. 4.   [2] Ibid. Vol. ii., p. 398.
[3] De la Beche, Geological Report.   [4] Dr. Boase. Davies Gilbert's Hist. Cornw., vol. iv., p. 47.

ANCIENT ROADS AND TRACKS.

The principal road into this parish is one we have described (Hist. of Trigg, Vol. i, p. 587) as entering it from the parish of Minster. It breaks the boundary of St. Teath at a place called " Cocks," and extends through the parish for a distance of five miles. This is the great road from the north-east described (ibid Vol. i, p. 484) as proceeding through the parish of St. Endellion to Plain Street, and (ibid v. iii, p. 8) extending thence through the parish of St. Minver to Pentire and the Roman Station near Padstow Harbour.

Another great thoroughfare entered St. Teath at Knight's Mill from the parish of Lanteglos (Hist. of Trigg, v. ii, 233), and passing St. Teath Church Town, entered St. Kew at Great Treveran (ibid Vol. ii, p. 81). At St. Teath Church Town a road branched off and passing in a westerly direction over Cheyney Downs crossed the great north-east road near Hendra and passed through Mid-Hendra to Port Gavern. The latter part of this road and a portion of the great north-east road are now extensively used in the conveyance of slates from Delabole Quarry to Port Gavern for shipment (ibid Vol. i, p. 484).

MEETING HOUSES OF DISSENTERS.

Wesleyan Methodists.—The earliest Meeting House in this parish was one erected upon a piece of ground at Pengelly, on a tenement called Cudlip's tenement there, which had been purchased by Robert Bake of Delaboll, Gent., of John Woollocombe of Roborough, Co. Devon, Esq., whereof the said Robert Bake, by indenture dated 13th February 1806[1] conveyed to Michael La Beaume of Botreaux Castle, Gent., Nicholas Male of St. Teath, Yeoman, and others, a piece of land measuring forty feet in length and twenty-seven feet in breadth, together with the building or house, then lately erected thereon, in trust for the people called Methodists according to the limitations of the model trust deed of that society dated 28th Feby. 1784. By the deaths of all the other trustees the aforesaid Nicholas Male became, eventually, the surviving trustee, and, to preserve the continuance of the said trusts, by indenture dated 31st July 1854[2] conveyed the said premises to Francis Garland and others. The building referred to, having become insufficient for the purposes of the Society, has been converted into a Sunday School, and a new and more commodious Meeting House has been built upon

---

[1] Rot. Claus. 46th Geo. III. Part 7, m. 1.　　[2] Inrolled in Chancery 23rd January 1855, Rot. Claus. 1855, Part 8.

a piece of land measuring eighty-nine feet in length and forty-six feet in breadth, situate in the village of Pengelly, granted, in consideration of the sum of £30, by deed dated 28th May 1869, by Joseph May Hawkey to George Martyn and several others, upon the same trusts as are contained in another model deed of the Wesleyan Methodists dated 3rd July 1832. This new building will seat 400 persons, and there are forty-five registered members attached to it.

United Methodist Free Churches.—Church Town.—By deed, dated 29th August 1815,[1] Moses Amy of St. Teath, House Carpenter, granted to Robert Pearse of Camelford, Clothier, and several others, a piece of ground in the Church Town of St. Teath, thirty-four feet in length and twenty-four feet in breadth, to be held in trust, according to the usual limitations of the Trust deed of the people called Methodists. Upon the schism in the Wesleyan body, however, the building erected on this land was carried over by the trustees to the Wesleyan Methodist Association, and is now possessed by the United Methodist Free Churches body, who have converted it into a Sunday School, having, in consideration of the sum of £36, obtained, by deed dated 20th April 1869, from Elias Martyn and Victoria his wife, the grant of a messuage, or dwelling house, &c., in the said village of St. Teath, which is vested in John May and eight others upon the same trusts as are contained in the United Methodist Free Churches model deed, dated 27th January 1842. The new buildings erected on this site will seat about 300 persons, and there are about eighty registered members of the Society attached to it.

Pengelly.—On 26th March 1842, a Chapel, then lately erected at Pengelly, was registered in the Archdeaconry Court of Cornwall by Walter Treleaven of Lanlivery, for the Wesleyan Methodist Association.

By Indenture dated 4th June 1865, John Smith of St. Stephen's in Brannell, Yeoman, being seized of an estate of inheritance in a field called the "Homer Stone's Ground," situate in Pengelly, conveyed to Thomas Greenwood of St. Teath, Yeoman, and others, in consideration of the sum of £131, a certain portion of the said field, containing by admeasurement twenty-four yards of land, to hold to them upon the trusts specified in the model deed of the people called the United Methodist Free Churches.[2] Upon this site a building was soon afterwards erected, which will seat 550 persons, and there are seventy registered members of the Society attached to it.

Treligga.—By Indenture dated 31st December 1829, George Martyn of Helland, in the parish of St. Teath, conveyed to Thomas Pope Rosevear of Boscastle, Merchant, Nathaniel Northey of Treligga, Yeoman, and others, in consideration of the sum of £5, a piece of land containing fifty-two feet in length and thirty-one feet in breadth, situate in the village of Treligga, to hold on the usual trusts of the people called Methodists. Upon this land a Meeting House was erected, and like that abovementioned at St. Teath,

---

[1] Rot. Claus. 56th Geo. III, Part 19, No. 3.
[2] Rot. Claus. 1865, Part 72, No. 2. Fine levied 24th June same year.

Plate LIII.

PLAN OF St TEATH CHURCH.

Fig. 1.

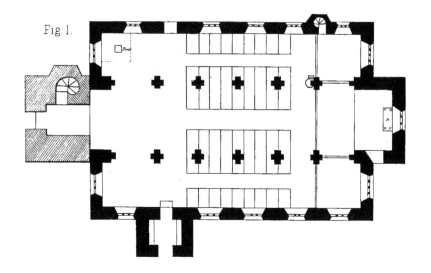

PLAN OF TEMPLE CHAPEL.

Fig. 2.

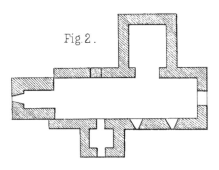

SCALE
10   0   10   20   30   40   50   60 FEET

Trans. Norman. ....
Third Pointed
Modern ....

was, in the same circumstances, carried over by the trustees to the Wesleyan Methodist Association, and is now vested in the United Methodist Free Churches body. The building will seat seventy persons and there are four registered members.

. *Bible Christians—Treligga.*—On 28th September 1820, a house in the occupation of Thomas Burt, in the village of Treligga, was registered in the Archdeaconry Court of Cornwall as a place of meeting for Brianites, now called "Bible Christians." This, or another building, had become vested in Abraham Bastard and Henry Langdon, both of St. Teath, Yeomen, for a term of 500 years, who, by Indenture dated 28th March 1859, under the description of "all that piece of ground containing 470 square feet, parcel of a certain tenement situate in the village of Treliggoe, known by the name of Bastard's Tenement, with a Chapel or Meeting House erected thereon," conveyed the same to Digory Baker, Roger Hayne, and others, for the residue of the said term upon the special trusts of the model deed of the people called Bible Christians. This building is said to have been erected in 1836, and will seat seventy persons. There are two registered members only attached to it.

Medrose.—By Indenture dated 30th June 1835, Thomas Rickard Avery, therein described, granted to Thomas Libby of St. Teath, Yeoman, a piece of land situate in Medrose, containing forty feet in length and twenty-two feet in width, parcel of a field called Higher Little Meadow, for the term of eighty years. And the said Thomas Libby, by Indenture dated 17th June 1836, granted the said piece of ground with the house, chapel, or building then lately erected thereon, to George Hocken of St. Tudy, Yeoman, and others, to hold to them, their heirs, executors, and assigns for the remainder of the said term, upon the trusts specified in the model deed of the people called Bible Christians, dated 8th August 1831, and enrolled in Chancery.[1] A new building was erected upon this site in 1863, which will seat 250 people, and there are seventy registered Members attached to it.

Church Town.—By Indenture, dated 1st March 1833, between John Martyn, Gent., of the first part, Richard Philp, Gent., of the second part, and Thomas Libby of the third part. A piece of land, being parcel of a field called Homer New Park, in St. Teath, was conveyed to the said Thomas Libby for the residue of a term of 1000 years. Upon this site in 1835 a Meeting House was built for the use of the Members of the Bible Christian Society, and by Indenture, dated 25th June 1846, the aforesaid Thomas Libby assigned the said chapel with its appurtenances, for the residue of the said term, to Thomas Whale Garland, Dissenting Minister, and Edward Hocken, Yeoman, both of Michaelstow, in trust for the uses prescribed for the people called Bible Christians.[2] This building will seat 150 persons, and there are 30 registered Members.

On 8th September 1823, a house in the village of Dilemeur was registered by Richard Andrew as a place of meeting for Brianites.

---

[1] Rot. Claus. 1862. Part. 47, No. 1.   [2] Inrolled in Chancery, 14th March 1862. Rot. Claus. 1862. Part. 47, No. 2.

We cannot be surprised at, and have not far to seek the causes of, the rapid growth of dissent in this parish. The development of the Delabole Slate Quarries had the effect of bringing together large populations in the villages of Pengelly and Medrose, which are in the immediate vicinity of the quarries, and distant from the parish Church three miles, without any provision, whatever, having been made for the ministration of the Ordinances of the Church there. The village of Treligga, also, which is another great centre of dissent, is still more distant from the parish Church, and equally destitute of Church Ordinances.

THE RECTORY AND VICARAGE.

This Benefice anciently belonged to the Bishops of Exeter, one of whom, at a very early date, founded two prebends or portions in the parish Church. On Saturday next after the feast of the Assumption of the Blessed Virgin Mary Bishop Bronescombe in the twelfth year of his episcopate (1269) assigned a Vicarage, to which he appropriated all the altalage and small tithes,. and the glebe, which was of the value of 2s. per annum, the vicar for the time being to bear all the burdens due and accustomed.[1] The advowson of the Vicarage in 1258 was vested in the Priory of Bodmin, in which year upon the presentation of the Prior and Convent, Warine de Byvile, Priest, was admitted thereto. They never made, however, another presentation, for the advowson of the Vicarage, as well as the rectorial tithes, became vested in the Bishops of Exeter. Bishop Grandisson collated Simon de Kari in 1333, from which date to the present time, whenever a vacancy has occurred in the Church, the Bishop has collated thereto.

. At the time of Pope Nicholas's taxation, 1288-1291, the Prebends were held respectively by Master Osbert and Master William de Wymondesham, as appears from the following valuation.—

		£ s. d.	Tenths. s. d.
Teth'	Prebendum Magistri Osberti ...	... 4 10 0	... 9 0
hñd pl'ra	Prebendum Magistri W. de Wymondesham	... 4 10 0	... 9 0
	Vicar Ejusdem	... 1 0 0	

In 1341 the ninth sheaf, the ninth fleece, and the ninth lamb of the Church of "Sancta Tetthe" were taxed at £10, and so sold to Warine Carkyon, John Broun, and Nicholas Treonek.[2] Of fifteenths there were none. It would seem from these valuations that the rectorial tithes were vested in the two Prebendaries or Portioners, but this does not appear to agree with Wolsey's valuation of 1535,[3] which shews that, irrespective of the two Prebends, the profits of the rectory were appropriated to the Cathedral of Exeter.—

[1] Bishop Bronescombe's Reg., fo. 42.   [2] Inq. Nonarum, p. 345.   [3] Valor Ecclesiasticus, vol. ii, p. 401.

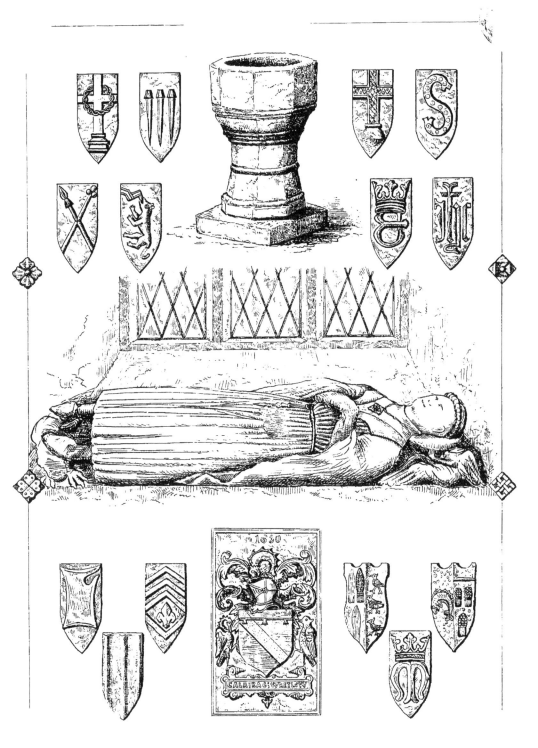

Tetha.—Profictuum proveniens de rectoria ibidem non redditur hic eo quod appro-} nihil.
priatum est ecclesiæ Cathedrali Exoniensi et remanet inde valore suo }

Vicaria ibidem valet per annum tam in decimis majoribus quam minoribus } xijli.
cum agistamento glebæ ultra viij⁵ ix⁴ ob. antiquitus solvit pro sinodalis }

Decima inde	-	-	-	- xxiiij⁵
Prebendum ibidem valet per annum	-	-	-	- vjli x⁵
Decima inde	-	-	-	- xiij⁵
Prebendum ibidem valet per annum	-	-	-	- vjli x⁵
Decima inde	-	-	-	- xiij⁴

The Incumbent of the rectorial tithes at this date was William Leveson,[1] Chancellor of the Cathedral, who, by Indenture dated 26th June (blank) Henry VIII, demised them to Richard Bennet for a term of twenty-one years.

In the early part of the reign of Queen Elizabeth, the prebends were held in farm by Christopher Cock of Camelford, Gent., at the rent of £13 6s. 8d. per annum. This term ended 1563, when, in consideration of the payment of a fine of £26 13s. 4d., being four years' rent, by lease dated 18th February 1563-4, one portion, being that which had been formerly held by William Leveson, was granted for a term of twenty-one years, at the annual rent of £6 13s. 4d., to John Frank, Cecilia his wife, and Elizabeth their daughter.[2] On 27th July 1583, there was a grant to Theophilus Adams and Robert Adams, their heirs and assigns for ever, of, *inter alia*, all those lands, tenements, oblations, obventions, tithes and profits lying being and arising within the parishes of St. Ethe and Endellion, before this given and granted, limited, and appointed to sustain divers prebends or priests in the Churches of St. Ethe and Endellion.[3] The Messrs. Adams were merely agents for the sale of the crown lands, and not having disposed of these premises, the grant must have been surrendered, for in 1588 a similar grant was made to Edward Wymark of London, Gent., of, *inter alia*, all the tithes, &c., and also *the advowson and right of presentation* to the prebends of Endelyon and St. Ethe :[4] from which it would appear that the prebends were not, at this time, dissolved. On the 22nd December 1590, a like grant was made to William Tipper and Robert Dawe, of London, Gentlemen,[5] but no sale would seem to have been effected, for, in 1607, King James, on account of the good and faithful services of Thomas Areskin (Erskine) Kut., Viscount Fenton, Captain of the Guard, granted to George Johnson of London, Merchant, and Edmund Bostock of London, Gent., *inter alia*, the portion, or prebend, of St. Ethe, which had been in the tenure of Richard Bennett, and afterwards demised to John Frank, his wife and daughter; and also the other part, or portion, of the prebend, then or late in the tenure of the said Richard

---

[1] William Leveson held this Prebend in 1536 and 1547. He was a nephew of Bishop Vesyey, by whom, on 22nd December 1537, he was collated to the Chancellorship of the Cathedral. (Aug. Off. Cert. No. 9).

[2] Augmentation Office, Particulars of Leases, Cornw. Roll 3, No. 9.

[3] Rot. Pat., 25th Elizab. Part 4, m. 7.   [4] Rot. Pat. 30th Elizab. Part 7, m. 7.

[5] Rot. Pat. 33rd Elizab. Part 9, m. 25.

Bennett, which same prebends, it is stated, were of the annual value of £13 6s. 6d.[1] In 1618, however, the rent for the two prebends was paid to the crown by Ralph Dawson, S.T.P.,[2] as it continued to be in 1630.[3]

Soon after this date it is probable that the rectorial tithes became annexed to the estate of Trehannick, which, in 1640, was possessed by the Carminow family, and with that estate passed to the family of Beale. William Beale, in 1712, by his will devised, *inter alia*, to his son, Mathew Beale, Trehannick and Trehannick Mills, together with the prebend, sheaf, rectory, impropriation and chancel of the parish Church of St. Etha, to be held in tail male. Trehannick afterwards passed to Samuel Lyne of Launceston, Gent., in the partition of whose estate between his three grandaughters and coheirs Trehannick and the great tithes of St. Teath fell to the share of Elizabeth daughter of Edmund Cheyne of Launceston, Gent., the eldest coheir, who married George Fursdon of Fursdon, co. Devon, Esq., and had a daughter named Elizabeth Penelope. This lady in 1786 married John Lyon of Exeter, Gent., who, in conjunction with the trustees under his marriage settlement, in 1798 sold Trehannick to Nicholas Male of St. Teath,[4] Gent., but the rectorial tithes were reserved, and in 1840 when the tithes were commuted into an annual rent charge, George William Lyon, Esq., nephew of the said John, was the possessor of the sheaf tithe.

On the survey for the tithe commutation it was found that the total quantity of land chargeable with tithes was 4842a. 1r. 4p., viz.—

	a.	r.	p.
Arable	3461	3	7
Meadow	117	3	0
Pasture	999	2	27
Woodland	32	3	20
Orchard and Nursery Ground	10	0	4
Common land	220	1	0
	4842	1	4

The tithes of corn and grain arising from the lands of Trehannick and Trehannick Mill, containing 139 acres, were found to have been merged in the freehold. The small tithes and tithes of hay arising from the glebe lands, containing 33a. 0r. 6p., were also merged in the said lands.

It was also found that the undermentioned lands were covered from the render of small tithes and tithes of hay in kind by several prescriptive payments, to which payments the vicar for the time being was found to be entitled, viz.—

	£	s.	d.		a.	r.	p.
Delabole	5	0	0	...	341	1	28
Trevela	2	2	0	...	102	0	0
Treveans		12	0	...	81	0	0

[1] Rot. Pat., 5th James, Part 1.   [2] Ministers' Accounts, 16th James.
[3] Ibid. 8th Charles.   [4] See post under TREHANNICK.

Dannon Chapel	...	...	...	2 17 6	...	220	0	0
Helland	.	...	...	...	4 0	...	80	0	0
Roses	...	...	...	...	15 0	...	38	0	0
Beef Parks, Tynes, Adam's and Baker's, Beckon Tenement, Pope's Tenement, Worth Tenement, and Muffles	...	5 0	...	64	2	0
Higher Hendra	...	...	...	2 8	...	77	0	0
Trevelly Parks	...	...	...	2 0	...	27	0	0
Part of Delamere	..	...	...	6 8	...	39	0	0
					...			
				?2 6 10	...	1049	3 28[1]

The gross rent charge payable for all the tithes was—

To George William Lyon, Esq., Impropriator, in respect to
tithes of corn and grain, except as aforesaid 396 12 8
To the Vicar for the time being 240 0 0

£636 12 8[2]

And a further sum of £1 10s. to be paid to the Impropriator in lieu of the tithes of the corn and grain arising out of the glebe lands when not in the occupation of the said Vicar himself, or a proportionate part for any portion not in the occupation of the said Vicar.

The abovementioned George William Lyon, by his will, dated 12th May 1843,[3] bequeathed all his real and personal estate to certain trustees for sale, who, in 1855, demised the Sheaf Tithe of St. Teath to Mr. Richard Parson of St. Austell, who, on his death on 11th October 1870, by his will, dated 21st December 1861, devised the said Tithes to his five daughters: Mary Ann Parson, Charlotte Elizabeth Parson, Jane Parson, and Emeline Parson, as tenants in common, who are the present possessors.

[1] It is stated—

							a.	r.	p.
Dannon Chapel Farm contains ..	..	..	..	..	..	234	3	8
Delabole Quarries ..	..	..	..	..	..	23	3	10
Church and Churchyard	..	..	..	..	..	..	1	0	16

[2] In addition to these sums the impropriator and the vicar for the time being are entitled to the tithes of certain lands in the parish of Lanteglos. See Hist. of Trigg, vol. ii., p. 300.

[3] Proved, P·C.C. 17th July 1854.

O[2]

Table shewing the devolution of the Great Tithes of St. Teath whilst in the possession of the Family of Lyne.

Those whose names are printed in CAPITALS held the Estate.

SAMUEL LYNE of Launceston⊤..
acquired of Mathew Beale
the Estate of Trehannick and
the Rectorial Tithes of St.
Teath. Will dated 5th Feb.
1735.

Edmund Cheyne of Launces-⊤.... Lyne.
ton. adm^{rd.} on behalf of his
daughters, to the estate of
Samuel Lyne, 6th Sep. 1737.

George Fursdon of Fursdon⊤ELIZABETH CHEYNE,	Joanna, dau.	Penelope, dau.	Benjamin⊤Elizabeth Ann, d.
co. Devon. Mar. Settl. dau. and coh.	and coh. mar.	and coh.	Lyon of of ...... Pusey,
dated 23rd and 24th Nov.	John Sawle.		Jamaica. living 1807,named
1753. Will dated 6th Jan.			in her grandson
1771.			George Benjamin
			Lyon's will.

ELIZABETH PENELOPE⊤JOHN LYON of Exeter,	EDMUND PUSEY⊤Charlotte Lewis	Elizabeth Ann	3 other
FURSDON, daughter son and heir, sold	LYON, 2nd son, of executrix to her	Lyon. Living	children.
mar. settl. dated 21st Trehannick to Nic-	Exeter. Will dated husband's will.	unmar. 1855	
and 22nd July 1786. holas Dale, 1798.	8th Sept. 1830.		
Died at Tiverton 1789, Died at Lisbon cir.	Prov. P.C.C. 20th		
and bur. at Cadbury. 1808.	May, 1831. Died		
Admo. granted 4th	4th Feb. 1831.		
July 1810, to Edmund			
Pusey Lyon.			

GEORGE BENJAMIN LYON,	EDMUND PUSEY LYON, son	GEORGE WILLIAM LYON, 2nd son,
only son and heir. Died at	and heir, Died unmar. Will	unmar. 1836. Died 20th June 1854.
Malta unmar. Will dated	dated 20th February 1832.	Will dated 12th May 1843, last cod.
25th November 1807. Prov.	Prov. P.C.C. 11th July 1834.	2nd July 1853. Prov. 17th July
P.C.C. 3rd November 1808.		1854, whose executors in Trust for
		sale sold the rectorial tithes of St.
		Teath in 1855, to Mr. Richard
		Parson of St. Austell.

THE VICARAGE.

As stated, Hist. of Trigg, v. iii, p. 96, the vicarage was assigned by Bishop Bronescombe in 1269, and from that date the advowson has been vested in the Bishops of Exeter. We have ust seen that in Wolsey's Taxation the value is stated to be £12 per annum, but in the valuation of Bishop Vesey in the following. year, it is returned at £11 10s. 0d. only. though the tenth is stated to be 12s. It is still rated in the King's Books at £12.[1] It possesses thirty-three acres of glebe, the description and boundaries whereof, as well as a deplorable account of the Vicarage house, we find given in a terrier dated in 1601.

[1] Oliver's Eccl. Antiquities, Devon and Cornwall, vol. ii, p. 151.

S₁. TEATH IN CORNWALL.

The vicarage house & ground of St. Teath is a mile & half quarter of a mile north from the Church. The glebe land about the howse is about six acres of arable land & three acres of moore & marish ground, bounded on the south side wᵗʰ a moore, or Downe, called Lanagan Downe, being the inheritance of William Cavell of St. Kew, Esquire, & bounded on the east, north, & west side wᵗʰ the Queene's highway.

Also, there is about other nyne acres of moore and heath ground, bounded on the Est side wᵗʰ the Queene's highway, and on the south side wᵗʰ a down called Trewynnan Down, whereof ar sondry lordes, and on the west side wᵗʰ a moore, or downe, called Taverner's down, supposed to be the land of Richard Taverner of St. Teath. And one the north side wᵗʰ a down called Delymere Downe, alias ffinche's Downe, supposed to be the landes of the foresaid Willyam Cavell, Esquire.

The Patron of the Benefice is the Right Honorable Lord Bishoppe of Exeter.

The implements to be therevppon left ar such as ar vnmoveable, being but few thinges, whereas the now Incumbent found there not any thing at all, but onely the bare bowses, and some of the howses but onely the bare walles, the howses vncouered & the Timber & Rooffe thereof taken away & burnt for fuell, and scarce one Dore to any one howse, & the sides of the windowes wanting, and the hedges & fences of the ground likewise in Extreme decay and Ruin, wᶜʰ ar now repayred & amended to the great costes & charges of this now Incumbent, to the somme of forty poundes & vpwardes, not vnknowne to the pishioners & others thereabout Inhabitinge.

p̃ me Thomam Cortier

1601. Vicarium de Teathe.

In a terrier dated in 1613, the boundaries of the glebe are more specifically described, though no further information is afforded respecting the benefice; but the following terrier, nearly a century later than the first, gives the then condition of the benefice in very interesting detail. —

CORNWᴸᴸ Sᵀ. TETH Vicaridge wᵗʰin the Deanarie of Trigg-Minor whereof a pfect Terrier, shewing how many Rooms be contayned in sᵈ Howse and how each roome is flored and p̃ted and whereof the Walls are made and what out-howses do appertayn thereunto ; also how many Acres of Glebe-land each field contayneth and how bounded and to whose Grounds they are adjoyned and how they be commonly knowen and distinguished as is here following truely witnessed and vnder the hands of the sᵈ Minister and the then Church Wardens Subscribed.

Sayd dwelling howse contayneth two larg vnder Rooms : viz, one Hall & one Kytchen decently p̃ted & both sᵈ Rooms handsomely Earthen flored. Two Chambers ouer which are yᵉ same length & breadth with yᵉ two vnder Rooms and both sᵈ higher Rooms formly planched & p̃ted with Dell-boards. Also there appertayneth herevnto one larg Barne and all the sᵈ Walles are with Stone decently and firmely builded.

The Orchard Nursery & Town-place, the whole one Acre. Three herb-gardens somewhat more than Quarter land the whole. Three fields vnderneath sᵈ Orchard & Gardens viz. Higher Bee-park, which is four Acres ; Lower Bee-park, one Acre : and the Moor-Meadow vnderneath them both, is half an Acre : all which afores^d are bounded on ye East with Lord Roberts tenem^t called Newall & on the South with Lanagan Downe.

One other field called the Church-park : Viz two acres & half that extendeth vp to the high way and is pted from the Bee-park with, or by, the three fores^d Gardens and bounded on the South-west with Lanagan Downe.

Three little fields more lying one above the other, called the Kitching parks ; all which contaynes only Two acres and half; that extend vp to the Highway and pted from s^d Bee-park wthabove s^d Orchard and Towne place, and are bounded on the East with Newall-Lane.

Two fields more called the Downe parks, alway estimated twelve acres and half & pted, with the Highway Lane from the s^d Church park & Kitching park & bounded on ye North East with ye Lord Roberts Downe-park & on the Northwest with ye Lord Mohuns Rough-park, and on the West with Langfords-Downes. This is a true and pfect Terrier of all belonging to the aboues^d vicarage of St. Teath according to advice received from the choycest and antientest of the Inhabitants of the said Parish, as is now attested, vnder our hands this

10th of March 16$\frac{79}{80}$

Sam. Veale, *Vic. ibidem.*
John Martyn, } *Churchwardens.*
Richard Tubb, }

[Addressed] For M^r ffra Blight,
    Merchant in
    Bodmyn.

Another Terrier, dated 20th October 1727, describes the Vicarage House and Glebe lands generally as above, and gives the following additional particulars as to the customs of the parish, some of which are very peculiar.

The surplice fee for marriage by Banns is one shilling, by License 5^s. Easter Offerings two pence for each person above 16 years old. Churchings of Women 1^s. Burials 1^s. Mortuaries none. The tithes of Coppice wood, Furse wood, grass, or Hay, Wool, Lambs, Apples, Hops, Garden stuff, Calves, Milk, Pigs, Geese, Honey, Eggs, Nurseries of Trees, Colts, and the tithe of depasturing of Barren Cattle, and all other titheable matter and things are due to the Vicar in kind, excepting only the tithe of corn which are due to the Impropriator. Trewalder Grounds, lying in the Parish of Lanteglos. that is the ground on the north side of the lane leading from the said village of Trewalder to Lanteglos Church, and consisting of 50 acres or upwards, pay tithes of grass in kind to the Vicar of St. Teath when the whole or any part thereof is mowed.

The pretended customary payments for particular estates within the said parish in lieu and in discharge of Tithes in kind are: Mr. Taverner's Trevilly Parks, which pay 2^s yearly. Mr. John Philips pays 6^s 8^d for his estate in Delamere. Richard Watts 2^s 8d^d for Hendra Park. Nicholas Philips 12^s for Treveans. Mr. Pitt 5^s for the Manor of Donnydizel. Mr. William Porter 4^s for Helland. Mr. Trevannion £5 for Donnyboule. Mr. Nicholls estate of Roses 8^d and Braddons Tenement lying in Trewinnel 6^s 8^d. All and each of these are said to be due and payable at Easter. On Trevela the Vicar has two Bullocks' pasture throughout the year. Mr. Pitts Donny Chappel, when in Tillage, pays four pence for each acre to the Vicar, and if the whole or any part thereof be mowed the tithe of the grass is due to the said Vicar in kind, and when the said Estate of Donny Chappel is neither tilled nor mowed the Vicar hath two Bullocks' pasture throughout the year in lieu of all other tithes in kind.

The Repairs of the Church and fences of the Churchyard are chargeable on the Parishioners and the Repairs of the Chancel on the Impropriator. The Clerk is appointed by the Vicar and the Sexton by the Parishioners.[1]

The Vicarage house, as stated above, being a mile and more distant from the parish Church, a new house was erected in 1821, on the west side of the churchyard, on three or four quillets of land purchased for the purpose by the Governors of Queen Anne's Bounty.

INSTITUTIONS TO THE PREBENDS OF ST. TEATH.

Unknown - -	William de Dysiman, Portioner.
1264 Translation of St. Thomas	Mr. Roger, called Barrett,[2] was admitted to the Portion of the Church of Sancta Thettha, which was held by Mr. William de Dysiman.
1270 Day of St. Francis the Bishop -	Peter de Tylleton, Chaplain to the Bishop,[3] was collated to a Portion of the Church of St. Tethe.
Unknown - -	Roger de Okeston.
1277 3rd Nones of April - -	Richard de Grangiis, Subdeacon and Chamberlain to the Bishop, was collated to a Prebend in the Church of St. Tethe which had been held by Roger de Okeston.[5]
Unknown - -	H. de Cristinestow.
1277 3rd Nones of May - -	Mr. William de Wymondesham, Subdeacon,[6] was collated to that Portion of the Church of St. Tethe which was held by H. de Cristinestow.
Unknown - -	Mr. Thomas de Wymondsham.
1277 Sunday next after the Ascension	Mr. William de Myddleton[7] was collated to the Prebend in the Church of St. Tethe vacant by the resignation of Mr. Thomas de Wymondesham.

[1] These Terriers are preserved in the Bishop's Registry at Exeter.
[2] Bishop Bronescombe's Reg., fo. 34.   [3] Ibid, fo. 45.   [4] Ibid, fo. 70.
[5] On Tuesday after the feast of St. Dionisius 1278, Richard de Grangiis resigned the Church of St. Michael of Clyst Somerton, and that moiety which he held of the Church of St. Teath, and was, the same day, admitted to the Church of Wyk in Cornwall (Week St. Mary?) upon the presentation of Richard de Albo Monasterio.
[6] Ibid, fo. 72.   [7] Ibid, fo 89.

		Mr. Osbert.[1]
1330	-	Vacant by Geoffry Lucy.
Unknown	-	Mr. Robert .... (? Osbert.)
Unknown	-	John Dalton.[2]
Unknown	-	W. Sergeous.[3]
1380 July 21	-	Mr. William Hendre, rector of Withiel,[4] was collated to a Prebend in the Church of St. Tethe, vacant through the death of John de Dalton.
1434 Dec. 27	-	Thomas Lewisham, Chaplain,[5] was collated to a Prebend in the Church of St. Tethe.
Unknown	-	Robert Nimune or Numm.
1501-2 June 16	-	Henry Aynesworth was collated to a Prebend in the Church of St. Tethe vice Robert Nimune or Numme.[6]
Unknown	-	John Clement.[7]
Unknown	-	William Luson (Leveson).[8]
Unknown	-	William Harman.[9]

INSTITUTIONS TO THE VICARAGE OF ST. TEATH.

1258 Morrow of the Invention of Holy Cross - - Warinus de Byvile, Priest,[10] was admitted to the Vicarage of St. Tethe on the presentation of the Prior and Convent of Bodmin.

1278 Day of St Agnes the Virgin Sir William de Nethe[11] was collated to the Vicarage of St. Tethe.

1333 February 27th Simon de Kari, Priest,[12] was collated to the Vicarage of St. Tethe.

Unknown - - John de Suttor.[13]

[1] Mr. Osbert and Mr. William de Wymundham are named as Prebendaries in the Taxation of the Bishops of Lincoln and Winchester 1294, (Bp. Bronescombe's Register).

[2] It appears from the Subsidy Roll of 1380 of an assessment of 16ᵈ in every mark from all Clerks, granted in the Archdeaconry of Cornwall, that John Dalton then held a prebend in the Church of St. Teath which Mr. Robert had held before, and he was assessed 9ˢ upon a stipend of £4 10s. (Sub. Roll. Clergy. $\frac{24}{4}$)

[3] This name is found in the Subsidy Roll cited above as holding the prebend which had formerly been held by W. de Wymundesham, and he was assessed at the same amount as John Dalton. He was doubtless the same person as William Sergaux, who, at that time, held the Prebend afterwards called Marny's Prebend in the Church of St. Endellion. (See Hist. of Trigg, vol. i., p. 500).

[4] Bishop Brentingham's Reg., vol. ii., fo. 60,
[5] Bishop Lacy's Reg., fo. 127.   [6] Rot. Pat. 17th Henry VII, Part 2, m. 13.
[7] John Clement appears as one of the prebendaries of St. Teath in Bishop Vesey's Valuation of 1536.
[8] Hist. of Trigg, v. iii, p. 96, 97.   [9] William Harman held the other Prebend in 1547 (Aug. Office, Cert. 9.)
[10] Bishop Bronescombe's Reg. fo. 6.   [11] Ibid, fo. 91.   [12] Bishop Grandisson's Reg. fo. 27.
[13] John de Suttor is named as Vicar of St. Tetha in 1380, and paid the benevolence of twenty groats assessed upon all Priests. (Sub. Roll, 4th Richard II, Clerical. $\frac{24}{5}$)

Unknown	-	John Kelly.[1]
1411 Oct. 19th	-	John Colle, Chaplain, was collated to the Vicarage of St. Tethe, vacant by the resignation of John Kelly, the last Vicar.
1450 April 15th	-	Thomas Coll, Chaplain,[2] was collated to the Vicarage of St. Tethe, vacant by the resignation of John Coll, Clerk, the last Vicar.
Unknown	-	Thomas Bryaunt.[4]
Unknown	-	John Person.[5]
1519 Jan. 24th	-	William Mann, Chaplain,[6] was collated to the Vicarage of St. Tethe, vacant by the death of John Person, the last Vicar.
Unknown -	-	William Maynewe.
1522 June 21st	-	Richard Manchester, Chaplain,[7] was collated to the Vicarage of St. Tethe, vacant by the resignation of William Maynewe, last Vicar.
1528 November 29th		John Batyn, Chaplain,[8] was collated to the Vicarage of St. Tethe, vacant by the resignation of Richard Manchester, last Vicar.
1552-3 February 10th		Nicholas Daniell[9] was collated.
1554 September 27th		Thomas Care[10] was collated.
1556 May 28th	-	Sir Robert Hyndre[11] was collated to the Vicarage of St. Tethe.
1573 January 15th		John Penkevell, Clerk,[12] was collated to the Vicarage of St. Teath, vacant by the death of the last Incumbent.
1586 June 28th	-	Thomas Courtier, Clerk,[13] was collated to the Vicarage of St. Teath, vacant by the resignation of Thomas [John] Penkevill, Clerk, last incumbent.

[1] John Kelly, Vicar of the Church of Seynt teth, in January 1384-5 sued John Bailly of Wyngate in a plea of trespass at Seynt teth by breaking into a certain Close there and removing a certain horse. (De Banco Roll, 8th Rich. II, Hil. m. 294). The case was still pending 18 months afterwards (Ibid. 9th Rich. II, Trinity, m. 309). In 1387 we find him sued by John Whitenhed and Thomasine his wife on a plea why he had taken at Seyntetha 40 sheep belonging to the same Thomasine of the value of 10 marks. (Ibid. 11th Rich II, Trinity, 138.)

[2] Bishop Stafford's Reg. fo. 136. John Colle is mentioned as Vicar of St. Teath 28th June 1441 (Bp. Lacy's Reg. fo. 206). John Colla was Chaplain at Advent between 1400 and 1407. (Sub. Roll, Cler. $\frac{2}{\frac{s}{18}}$

[3] Bishop Stafford's Register. fo. 262.

[4] On 15th June 1466 John Bryaunt, Vicar of St. Teth, was juror on an Inquisition concerning the right of presentation to one of the Prebends of Endellion. (Bishop Booth's Reg. fo. 60.)

[5] On 5th May 1489 John Person, Vicar of St. Tethe, was juror on an Inquisition concerning the right of presentation to the Church of Lesnewith (Booth's Reg., fo. 119,) as he was also on 19th May 1498 concerning the patronage of Tintagel (Redmayn's Reg., fo. 24.)

[6] Bishop Veysey's Reg., fo. 2.   [7] Bishop Veysey's Reg. fo. 12.

[8] Ibid, fo. 39. This Vicar is mentioned in Bishop Veysey's Valuation of 1536.

[9] Bishop's Certificates, Aug. Office. But the collation is not found recorded in the Bishop's Register.

[10] Ibid.   [11] Bishop Turberville's Reg. fo. 11. Bur. at St. Teath, 1573.

[12] Bishop Bradbridge's Reg. fo. 17.

[13] Bishop Wootton's Reg. fo. 26. Bur. at St. Teath, 2nd September 1604. Inventory of his effects in the Probate Court at Exeter, dated 16th October 1604.

P

1604 November 10th   John Nichell, Clerk, M.A.,[1] was admitted to the Church of St. Tethe, vacant by death of Thomas Courtier, last Incumbent, upon the presentation of Richard Nichell of the parish of St. Tethe, Gent., for this turn the true patron by the grant of the Lord Bishop of Exeter.

1605 September 26th John Cole, Clerk,[2] was collated to the Vicarage of St. Tethe, vacant by the death of John Nichell, last Incumbent.

1609 June 9th   -   Thomas Symmes, Clerk,[3] was collated to the Vicarage of St. Tethe, vacant by the resignation of John Cole, last Incumbent.

1645 August 19th -   William Adams, Clerk, M.A.,[4] was collated to the Vicarage of St. Teath, vacant by the death of Thomas Syms, last Incumbent.

1660 March 4th   -   Samuel Veale, M.A.,[5] was collated to the Vicarage of St. Teath.

1704 Sept. 19th   -   Thomas Mayo, Clerk,[6] was collated to the Vicarage of St. Teath, vacant by the death of Samuel Veale, last Incumbent.

1720 October 3rd -   Thomas Billington, Clerk, M.A.,[7] was collated to the Vicarage of St. Teath. vacant by the death of Thomas Mayo, Clerk, last Incumbent.

1723 April 2nd   -   William Whiteborne, Clerk, M.A.,[8] was collated to the Vicarage of St. Teath, vacant by the resignation of Thomas Billington, Clerk, last Incumbent.

1737 October 27th -   Benjamin Shipman, Clerk, B.A.,[9] was collated to the Vicarage of St. Teath, vacant by the death of William Whiteborne, last Incumbent.

1779 August 7th   -   Sampson Harris, Clerk, B.A.,[10] was collated to the Vicarage of St. Teath, vacant by the cession of Benjamin Shipman, Clerk, last Incumbent.

---

[1] Bishop Cotton's Reg. fo. 80.

[2] Ibid. Matriculated at Exeter College Oxford, 3rd November 1592. Esquire's son, co. Devon, aged 14.

[3] Ibid, fo. 91. Adm° of the goods, &c., of Thomas Symms, Vicar of St. Teath, granted, 27th April 1648, to his son Nathaniel Symms of Foy. The value of the Inventory was only £4 5s. 0d. Phillipp wife of Thomas Symes, Vickar, bur. 1636. John son of Thomas Symes, Vickar, bur. 1639. Thomas Symmes, Vicar, buried 1645. St. Teath P.R.

[4] Bishop Hall's Reg., fo. 61.

[5] Bishops' Reg., N.S., Vol. i, fo. 10. Matriculated at Exeter Coll., Oxford, 6th Dec. 1639, aged 17, son of Rev. Walter Veale, of Iddesleigh, co. Devon. Mr. Samuel Veale and Mrs. Johan Blake mar. 1654. Mr. Samuel Veale, Vicker, buried 23rd Sept, 1704. P.R.

[6] Ibid. Vol. iv, fo. 111. Son of John Mayow of Michaelstow, Gent., Matric. at Hart Hall, Oxford, 26th May 1691, aged 18. Mr. Thomas Mayow, Vicar, bur. 9 Sept. 1720. P.R.

[7] Ibid. Vol. v, fo. 134.

[8] Ibid. Vol. vi, fo. 4. Matriculated at Exeter Coll., Oxford, 3rd April 1707, aged 17. Son of Rev. Joseph Whiteborne.

[9] Ibid. Vol. vii, fo. 18. Buried at St. Teath 1790. P.R.

[10] Ibid. Vol. ix, fo. 158. Matric. at Exeter Coll., Oxford, 14th April 1773, aged 19. Son of Sampson, Harris of Probus, Gent.

1784 June 15th   -   Richard Eliott, Clerk,[1] was collated to the Vicarage of St. Teath, vacant by the death of Sampson Harris, Clerk, last Incumbent.

1785 February 12th-   Richard Eliott, Clerk,[2] was collated to the Vicarage of St. Teath, vacant by his own cession.

1795 December 30th   Jonathan Williams, Clerk,[3] was collated to the Vicarage of St. Teath, vacant by the death of Richard Eliott, Clerk.

1821 October 12th -   Joseph Fayrer, Clerk, M.A.,[4] was collated to the Vicarage of St. Teath, void by the death of Jonathan Williams, Clerk, last Incumbent.

1838 June 20th   -   Thomas Amory, Clerk, B.A.,[5] was collated to the Vicarage of St. Teath, void by the death of Joseph Fayrer, Clerk, last Incumbent.

PARISH CHURCH.

The Parish Church (Plate LI), which is entirely of Third Pointed date, except the tower, which was built in 1630, is dedicated to St. Tetha, one of the daughters of Brychan. It consists of a Sanctuary, disengaged, 10 ft. 7 in. × 15 ft. 6 in., on the south side of which is a priest's door. Chancel 11 ft. × 15 ft. 6 in.; Nave 61 ft. × 18 ft. 3 in.; two Chapels, north and south, each 12 ft. 9 in. × 13 ft.; North and South Aisles, each 33 ft. 9 in. × 13 ft.; South Porch and Western Tower (see Ground Plan, Plate LII, fig. 1).

The nave, which is of five bays, was pewed through four bays only. It had nine benches on each side, and the aisles contained the same number. Many of them have now been removed and square pews substituted. The western bay in the north aisle appears to have been separately benched.

The east window of the Chancel is of three-lights, cinquefoil, with elongated quatrefoils in the head. In it is a circular piece of ancient glass exhibiting the sacred wounds. The east wall shews marks of a reredos within the splay of the window. There is a piscina in the south east corner, plastered over, and on the north side is an aumbry. The base of the Chancel screen remains in situ. Some parts of the Chapel screens also remain. That of the north chapel has well carved, boldly cut, linen pattern panels, in richly carved frames,

---

[1] Bishops' Reg. N.S., Vol. x, fo. 7. Matric. at Trinity Coll., Oxford, 24th March 1773, aged 17. Son of William Eliot, Gent., of Lostwithiel.

[2] Ibid, fo. 21.

[3] Ibid. Vol. x, fo. 143. Matric. at Pembroke Coll., Oxford, 23rd February 1770, aged 16, son of David Williams of Rhayader, co. Radnor, Pleb.

[4] Ibid, Vol. ix, fo. 121. Died 10th May 1838, aged 52. Buried at St. Teath, M.I., No. 20, p. 113.

[5] Ibid, Vol. xii, fo. 132. Son of Thomas Amory of Southmolton, Devon, Esq., Matric. at Wadham Coll., Oxford, 24th March, 1811, Aged 18.

P²

of Third Pointed work. North Chapel, east window four-light, cinquefoil, with tracery in the head. This window is newly glazed. North window three-light, cinquefoil, ogee, with cinquefoil tracery. In the openings are two escutcheons of arms: that on the western side, ar. a chev. sa. between three lapwings, impaling: sa., six mullets, 3, 2, and 1, pierced, ar. (See Plate LIII, lower angles). On the eastern side the same arms impaling ar. a chev. sa. between three annulets, vert.[1] On the eastern splay of the window is an oblong nich with depressed ogee head, and there was a nich in the face of the east wall now built up, but the base, or bracket, is still apparent. On the south side is a small piscina, or possibly a squint, now plastered over. From this chapel opened the door to the rood loft staircase. In this Chapel are now placed some finely carved bench ends, which would seem to have formed the stalls in the choir. They are somewhat narrower than the usual type, and formed the fronts of the stalls. On one is an escutcheon charged with three garbs, impaling, three birds, not quite in pale. On a second shield we find a dolphin embowed, impaling: three garbs 2 and 1, and a chief. (Peveril of Hamatethy.) (Plate LIII.) There are four windows in the north aisle, similar to that in the Chapel, and a north door. The second window from the west has in its tracery two escutcheons of arms: the western: ar. a chev. sa. betw. three annulets vert; and the other: sa. a cock ar., legged or, pecking at a branch of acorns of the last. (Plate LIII, upper angles). Part of the western bay is now railed off as a baptistery, and thither the font, which is octagonal on a square base, (Plate LIII,) has been removed from its original position in the second bay between the north and south doors. The bench ends in the aisles are ornamented with shields, bearing crowned " M's " and the sacred monogram. Upon one, in the north aisle, are two shields, one charged with a Calvary cross, and upon the other the letter " S."[2] The roofs of this aisle and of the Chapel are of the cradle pattern and have particularly well carved bosses, mostly foliated.

The nave requires no particular remark except that the bench ends abutting on the middle passage, so far as they remain, are ornamented with shields, charged with emblems of the Passion. Over the rood beam are set up the tables of the Commandments, and between the tables the Royal Arms, with the date 1703, and the motto " Semper fidem." The last bay is filled by a hideous gallery. The roof is much disfigured.

In the south Chapel the east window is of five-light, cinquefoil, ogee. It is divided into two compartments embracing two lights each, the space over the middle light being filled with mullioned and transomed tracery. There is a piscina in the south wall plastered over. In the base of the window is a well cut grave stone in memory of

---

[1] C. S. Gilbert mentions that in the east window of the north aisle was, when he wrote, a shield charged with the arms of King Henry VII. Also five other shields, charged as follows: 1st, Mohun, ancient and modern, quarterly, and quartering Fitzwilliam, St. Aubyn, Lair, Beville, and Courtenay, impaled with Coad; 2, Mohun quartering Fitz-William, Lair and Beville, impaled with Courtenay; 3, Trevanion and Mohun quarterly; 4, ar. a chev. sa. between three birds, gu., impaling ar. three pommes; 5, the same coat impaling Bonville. The royal arms, and 1st, 2nd, and 3rd shields, are now lost. The 4th and 5th shields are inaccurately blazoned, they should be as in the text.

[2] The variety of design in the quatrefoils at the base of the bench ends is illustrated by the six little figures in the border of Plate liij.

DELABOLE SCHOOLS.
SILVANUS TREVAIL ARCHT.

Florence, the wife of Hugh Carew of Trevia who died in 1656. There is a window in each bay of the south aisle except that occupied by the door, and another at the west end. In the base of the easternmost window is a recumbent effigy of a man, the head supported by angels and at the feet two lions. It is much mutilated. The figure is represented as clad in an inner garment or shirt (which was painted red), fitting close around the throat, and over this, about the neck, is a knotted cord from which is suspended an ornament of a quatrefoil form. The outer garment is opened at the neck, the collar being turned back over the shoulders. It has loose hanging sleeves, like a surplice, and is girded at the waist, where it is gathered into plaits, and fastened by a knotted cord, the ends of which hang down on the right side. The vesture falls in graceful folds to near the ancle ; it was painted of a light brown, or amber, colour, and the hair of a rich brown, without a tonsure, but parted in the middle, and having short crisp curls all around. (See Plate LIII.) Between the first and second windows is set against the wall a slate slab, upon which is sculptured in low relief the figure of a woman holding a skull resting upon a thigh bone. In a lower compartment are two other figures of a man and woman. Around the margin is the following inscription : " Here lyeth the Bodye of Francis the wife of Phillipe Bennet of this Parrish, who was bvrved the xxx daye of October Anno Dom. 1636." On a band between the figures : " John Bennet o ⦂ o Elizabeth Bennett," and below the following lines :—

> In life shee Feared God
> In death shee showed the same,
> In life and death she did him praise
> And Bles his holy name.

The windows differ alternatively. The second from the door is three-light cinque-foil ogee, but the centre light is higher than the others, and in the tracery are two shields, in ancient glass, having the sacred monogram "I.H.S." and the letter " N." with a fleur-de-lis above the shield. In the window nearest the door is a shield charged with emblems of the Passion.

Two or three large pewes have been erected in and about the Chancel, of the time of Charles I, richly ornamented with arabesque work, as are also the panels of the pulpit : in the front panel of which are the arms of Carminow with crest and mantling, and, as supporters, on the dexter an eagle or, and sinister a hawke ppr. Motto: CALA ⦂ RAG ⦂ WHETLOW. Above the shield is the date 1630. (See Plate LIII.)

The porch measures 10 ft. by 9 ft. The outer doorway has a circular arch with hood moulding. The arch of the inner door is equilaterel, with continuous mouldings. The tower is of three flights, battlemented and pinacled.

The western door has a circular arch with square headed hood moulding. Upon the plinth are the words " Anno Domini," and upon the drop ends, 1630. The west window is of three-lights, similar to the aisle windows of the Church. Underneath the gallery is a bench from the north aisle, on the end of which are two shields, one charged with the spear and sponge in saltier ; and the other charged with a dog holding in his mouth a label. On the end of a smaller bench in the tower are two shields, one charged with a tilting shield, and the other between three chevronels in chief, and one in base, reversed, a fleur de lis. (See Plate LIII.)

There is a ring of five bells, thus inscribed :—

1. ROBERT STAINBANK FOUNDER LONDON. 1868.

2. The same as 1.

3. A. & R. 1756 PROSPERITY TO THE CHURCH OF ENGLAND.

4. The same as 1.

5. I TO THE CHURCH THE LIVING CALL & TO THE GRAVE DO SUMMON ALL 1756.

MONUMENTAL INSCRIPTIONS.

1. Against north wall of the Chancel, on a handsome marble tablet, set in a free stone frame of a Gothic pattern :

"To the memory of Rev. John Thorne who for thirty-two years was the faithful and beloved Pastor of this Parish, he departed this life on the 1st day of February 1818, in the 72nd year of his age

Also of Eleanor his wife, daughter of the Rev. James Wilkins, Vicar of Catcombe and Luxborough, in the county of Somerset, whose remains were interred at Okehampton in the county of Devon, where she died, on this 10th day of October 1830, in her 75th year.

In affectionate remembrance of his beloved Parents the Rev. Joseph Thorne, M.A., Vicar of Bishop's Nympton, in the county of Devon, has caused this tablet to be erected."

2. On a large flat slab in the floor, very much worn:

"Here lies the body of Margaret the daughter of Peter Dagge, which was buried the xxvi day of May 1612.

3. In north Chapel :

Here lyeth the body of William Phillips of Treveans, in this Parish, who was buired (sic) the 12th day of April 1712, in the 62nd year of his age.

> Annis maturus numerosâ ac Prole beatus
> Grave hic depono Mortalitatis Onus
> Et morior lubens, dum Christi in Nomine spero
> Hinc abiens Cœlo Tempus in omne frui."
> Resurgam.

4. In north aisle :

" Beneath This Stone lies the Body of Philip Robins of Trekee, in this Parish, who departed this life the 23rd of August 1802, in the 95th year of his age. A Man of Strict Integrity and Virtue."

5. Against the wall, circumscribed:

" Here lieth the body of Thomas Harris of Meadrose in this Psh who wass Buried 12th day of December in the year of our Lord 1670. Ætatis suo 56."

In the middle are 26 lines of doggerel.

6. Circumscribing a well cut stone, set in the splay of the sill of one of the windows of the south chapel:

"Florence the wife of Hugh Carew of Trevie wthin ye pish of Lanteglos by Camelford, Gent., was Buried ye 9th Nombr. 1656.[1]

> The father's joy, the Grandame's hope, one stone
> Now hides the Mother and her infants twain,
> The comfort they expected turn to mone,
> Their late delights becom heart-breaking paine.
> One transitorie things fixe not your loue
> For lasting ioys are only from aboue.

7. In south aisle, against the wall, a slate slab circumscribed:

Here lyeth the body of Hester the Wife of Humphry Harris of Meadrose, in this Parish, who was buried the 29th day of Octobr. 1670.

And in the middle:

> " Here lies inter'd a mayd, a wife, a mother
> virtue, loue, prudence, mixed each wth other,
> in each estate her duties, loue & care
> was shown to parents, husband, children deare.
> prayer was her practes, piety her pleasure,
> the world her pilgrimage and heaven her treasure.
> This lifes affliction vnto her made double,
> grief falling still on grief, & care on trouble ;
> all which shee with admired patience past
> and meagre death hath conquered death at last ;
> instead of which shee now is full possest
> of endlesse joye & everlasting rest."

8 In memory of Richard Craddock of Lower Hender, in this Parish, buried Feb. 19th 1704, aged 57.

Mary his Wife, buried Octobr 1st 1712, aged 74.

John their Son, buried March 1st 1704, aged 31.

And Elizabeth their daughter, buried August ye 8th 1705, aged 25.

> Here Age with Youth, Parents wth Children ly
> To Mind Survivors of Mortality.

[1] Florence the first wife of Hugh Carew, fourth son of Richard Carew, Author of the "Survey of Cornwall." Her two children died in infancy. (See Ped. Hist. of Trigg, Vol. ii, p. 367.)

9. Near this Place lyes Hendor the son of y⁰ Reu⁴ James Amy & Ꞁary his Wife, was Buried Ap. yᵉ 11ᵗʰ 1727, aged 14.

Also the Reu⁴ James Amy, Rectʳ of Ꞁinster & Forrabury, buried Ꞁarch The 19ᵗʰ 1736, aged 59.

Ꞁary his Wife, buried May yʳ 4ᵗʰ 1751, aged 74.

Ꞁary their Grandaughter, Buried December 31st, 1782 (?)

10. Here lies the body of Ann the wife of John Brown of Trelego in this P'sh, who was buried the 12ᵗʰ day of Iune 1763, in the 29ᵗʰ year of her age.

Also the body of Anne the Daughter of John and Anne Brown, who was buried here the 7ᵗʰ day of Iune 1760, aged 4 years.

11. In the north Chapel :
Sacred to the Ꞁemory of Ꞁattᵛ Trevan, late of Pengelly in this Parish, who left this world in full hope of a blessed Eternity August the 2ⁿᵈ 1809, aged 46.

12. In the splay of a window in the north aisle :
"In Ꞁemory of Richard Watts and Anne his Wife, of this Pⁿ, Anne was buried the 16ᵗʰ day of Nov., Anno Dom. 1759, aged 80 ; and Richard Watts was buried the 12ᵗʰ day of Iune, Anno Dom. 1763, aged 90."

13. "In Ꞁemory of William the son of Richard Watts and Anne his Wife, of this Parish, who was Buried the 7ᵗʰ day of Dec. Anno Dom. 1774, in the 70ᵗʰ year of his age.

Also, in Ꞁemory of Ꞁargaret the Wife of the said William Watts, of this Parish, who was Buried the 8ᵗʰ day of Novʳ, Anno Dom. 1786, In the 85ᵗʰ year of her Age."

14. Against the north wall circumscribed :
.... the Body of John Blake, who was buryed the 22ⁿᵈ day of Dec. (The remainder is hidden by a high pew.)

15. Against a pew in the middle passage of the nave :
"Here lyeth the Body of Elizabeth the Wife of Nicholas Phillipps of Newhall, who was buried the 13ᵗʰ day of February 1713, in yᵉ 27ᵗʰ yeare of her Age. And also the Bodyes of Elizabeth & Ꞁargery Phillipps, their children. Elizabeth was buried yᵉ 8ᵗʰ day of May 1712. Ꞁargery was buried yᵉ 8ᵗʰ day of June 1714.'

16. "Sacred to the Ꞁemory of Richard Watts of Hendra, in this Parish, who departed this life the 22nd Day of Sept. 1813, aged 71. Also, to the memory of Ann his daughter, the Wife of Richard .... of this Parish, who departed this life the 16ᵗʰ Day of January 1818, aged 33.

17. On a handsome slate tablet in the north aisle :
"Here lyeth the body of Humphry Harris, who was buried the 12ᵗʰ day of Ꞁarch, Ann. Domini 1687, ætatis 48.

Here lies my dust
but I do live above,
Earth's graue the rauen hid's
Heauen's Ark the Dove.
Sure both shall liue
this body shall arise
when dooms day comes
Earth's General Assize.
In memory of my husband dear
this Tomb
I have erected here.
Francis Harris.

18. In the tower, against the wall, around the margin of a slate slab, on which is incised a Calvary cross:

Heare lieth the Body of John Taverner, Gentelman, and too sonnes and too daughters, and buried the [blank[1]] of December Anno Domini 158[6.]

Painted underneath the arms of the cross: "Thomas Taverner."

19. Here lieth the body of Richard Dingle, of Lower Suffenton, in this Parish, who was buried 1st January 1741, aged 91.

In the Church Yard.

20 Here lies the body of Alice Honey, who died 7 May 1720.

How vain our wishes, fruitless our desires,
Which, like to Embrios, ere born expires.
Thus here a Husband flushed with hopes to see
Himself the Father of faire progeny.
But, ah! how soon his expectation's crost.
The mother dead, who longed for offspring lost.
To man there's nothing certain but the grave,
For hopes, as life, a sudden exit have.

20 Sacred to the memory of the Revd Joseph Fayrer, M.A., for 17 years Vicar of this Parish, who died May 10th 1838, aged 52.

21. On a slab against the wall of the Church:

[1] John Taverner, gen., was buried 3rd Dec. 1586. P.R.

Q

HERE. LYETH. THE. BODY. OF. ROBERT. BAKE. SON. OF. SAMYEL. BAKE.
WHO. WAS. BURIED. THE. XXX. DEAY. OF. IANUARY. 1686.
BUT. WHAT. CHEERE. VP. ALTHO. OVRE. SONNE. BEGONE.
ALTHO. HIS. BODY. MVST. BE. RACKE AND. TOREN.
WITH. FILTHY. BITTER. BITINGE. WORMES. OF. DUSTE.
AND. BE. CONSVM'D. AS. ALL. OVRE. BODIES. MVST.
YET. STILL. CHEERE. VP. CONFORTE. YOVRE. SELVES. IN. THIS.
THO. THE. BODY. DIED. THE. SOVLE. EMMORTALL. IS.
AND. NOW. IN. HEAVEN. MOST. IOYFOLLY. SHALL. SINGE.
O : GRAVE. WHERE. IS. THY. STRENGTH. DEATH. WHER. IS. THY. VICTORY.
AND. SOE. SHALL. REINE. IN. IM : MORTALLITIE .·.   FOR
WITH. GOD. ABOVE. FOR. ALL. E. TERNY. TIE :   ROBERT BAKE.

22. On an altar tomb :

Here lyeth the bodies of Moses and Elizabeth, son and Daughter of Sam. and Phillippa Bake, of this P'sh. Moses was buried the 11th of January 1732 aged 6 months. Elizabeth was buried the 22nd of May Anno Dom. 1748, in the 21st year of her age.

Here lies the Body of Jonathan Son of Robert and Elizabeth Bake of this P'sh who was buried the 4th day of Decr Anno Dom. 1754, in the 22nd Year of his age.

23. Sacred to the Memory of Samuel Bake of the Parish of Lanteglos, who departed this life the 8th day of May 1783, aged 45. Also, in memory of Mary his wife whe departed this life the 27th day of Feby 1816, Aged 69.

24. On an altar tomb :

Beneath this Stone lieth the body of Samuel Brown of this Parish, who was buried July 19th 1788, aged 57.

Also, in memory of Rebecca his wife who was buried March the 29th, 1791, aged 84.

25. On an altar tomb :

In memory of William Bant, of this Parish, who Departed this life the 4th day of May 1776, aged 78. Also, of Ann his wife, who Departed this life the 26th day of Decer 1778, aged 84. Also : of Ann their daughter, who departed this life the 24th day of March, 1748, aged 3 years. Also, of Ann the daughter of John and Lucy Bant, of this Parish, who Departed this life the 23rd day of May 1767, aged 5 weeks. Also, of William their son, who Departed this life the 18th day of Decmr 1770, aged 4 weeks. Also, of Mary the wife of Anthony Snell, of this Parish, and daughter of the above William and Ann Bant, who Departed this life ye 15th day of Jany 1784, aged 44. Also, of Lucy the wife of John Bant, of this Parish, who Departed this life Novr the 30th 1787, aged 57. Also, of John Bant, Gent., of Suffenton (and son of the above Willm & Ann Bant) who departed this life the 9th day of June 1822, in the 84th year of his age.

26. Against the Church wall :

To the memory of Lucy the Daughter of John and Elizabeth Bant, of Lower Suffenton, in this Parish. She departed this life May the 6th 1826, aged one year and eleven months

Also, to the Memory of Elizabeth Lucy, daughter of the aforesaid John and Elizabeth Bant, who departed this life June the 27ᵗʰ 1855, aged 27 years.

Also, of John Bant, father of the above named John Bant ; who departed this life Novʳ the 26ᵗʰ 1856, aged 91 years. Likewise, to the Memory of Mary Ann, daughter of the said John and Elizabeth Bant, who departed this life August the 15ᵗʰ 1857, aged 31 years.

27. Sacred to the Memory of Moses Male (Late of Pengelly in this Parish) son of Christopher and Ann Male, who departed this life Decʳ the 11ᵗʰ 1806, aged 29 years.

And John Male, who departed this life March the 16ᵗʰ 1812, aged eight years.

Also, of Miss Ann Male, who departed this life April the 6ᵗʰ 181-. Aged 29 years.

And Jane Male, who departed this life April the 20ᵗʰ 1812, aged two years.

28. Sacred to the Memory of John Male of the Parish of Tintagel, Gentⁿ, who departed this life on the 13ᵗʰ day of July 1807, aged 86 years.

In him the poor have lost a friend . . . . and to whom his memory will ever be precious.

29. Here Lies the body of Phillippa Wife of Christopher Male, who was buried the 19ᵗʰ day of June 1765, in the 21ˢᵗ year of her age.

Also, the body of John the son of Christopher and Phillippa Male, who was buried in his mother's grave.

30. In memory of John Male, late of this Parish, who departed this life on the 12ᵗʰ day of Octʳ 1873, aged 84 years.

31. In Memory of Nicholas Male, late of Treburget in this Parish. He departed this Life August the 23ʳᵈ 1830, aged 81.

Also, in Memory of Elizabeth wife of the said Nicholas Male. She departed this Life August the 30ᵗʰ 1819, aged 63.

32. On the base of a cross ;
M. S. Nicholas Male, who died June 1ˢᵗ 1871, aged 68.
Also, Catherine his wife, August 16ᵗʰ 1844, aged 50.

33. Sacred to the Memory of Catherine Male, Daughter of Nicholas and Ann Male of Trehannick, in this Parish, who died on the 30ᵗʰ day of April 1860, aged 60 years.

34. On an altar tomb :
Sacred to the Memory of Nicholas Male, Esqʳ, Late of Trehannick in this Parish. A Friend to the Labourer and a Benefactor to the Poor, Who quitted this mortal state on the 24ᵗʰ day of June 1817, aged 56 years.

Also, in Memory of Ann Male, the Wife of the said Nicholas Male, who died at St. Mabyn on the Twenty-seventh of February 1854, aged 88 years.

35. Here lies the Body of Nicholas Male, of this Parish, who was Buried the 16ᵗʰ day of September, Anno Domini 1789, in the 61ˢᵗ year of his age.

Q²

36. In Memory of Grace Tucker, late of this Parish, and Widow of Gideon Tucker of this Parish, whose Remains lie in the adjoining Grave. She departed this life on the 24th day of April 1814, aged 54 years.

37. On an altar tomb :
Here lies the Body of Thomas Kempthorne, of this P^{sh}, who was buried the 23rd day of March, Anno Domini 1758, Aged 84 years.
Also, the Body Elizabeth his wife who was buried the first Day of May 1762, aged 88 years.
Here also lies the body of Margaret Nicholl, who was buried the 29th Day of April 1741, aged 89 years.

> Christ is to us as life on Earth
> And Death to us is Gain,
> Because we trust thro' him alone
> Salvation to obtain.
> So brittle is the state of Man
> So soon it doth decay,
> So all the glory of the world
> Must pass and fade away.

38. Robert Bake died Feby. 24, 1825, aged 65.

39. On an altar tomb :
In Memory of Robert Bake, Gent., of Delabole Quarry, who by a Fall from his horse on the 16th Jany Died the 17th Jany 1830, aged 39 years.

> Lord solemnize each Trifling mind
> And help them Seriously to think,
> A vast eternity is near
> And every Soul is on the brink.

Also Hugh Lakeman, son of Robert and Ann Bake, died July the 16th 1824, aged six years.

39. In affectionate remembrance of Grace wife of John Amy of Roughpark, in this Parish, who departed this life 16th of Septemb^r 1867, aged 58 years.

40. Here lyeth the body of Alice wife of John Honey of this P^{sh}, who was Buried the 7th Day of May, Anno Domini 1720, Aged 35.

41. On an altar tomb :
Sacred to the Memory of Thos Martyn, late of Trecarn in the Parish of Tintagel, the son of George and Mary Martyn late of Hellanin in this Parish, who departed this life October the 1st 1803, in the 54th year of his age.
Also, Mary the wife of Thomas Martyn, daughter of John and Ann Symons, of the Parish of Michaelstow, who died the 30th of September 1822, aged 71 years.
Also, to the memory of Ann daughter of the aforesaid Thomas and Mary Martyn, who departed this life on the 29th day of December 1861, aged 75 years.

42. On an altar tomb :

Sacred to the memory of Joan, the daughter of Thomas and Mary Martyn of Trecarn in the Parish of Tintagel, who departed this life August the 7th 1828, aged 34 years.

We rest in Hope.

43. On an altar tomb:

Sacred to the memory of George Martyn, Late of Helland, in this Parish, who departed this life the 28th day of March 1796, aged 81 years.

Also, Mary Martyn, his Wife, who departed this Life the 31st day of Augt 1794, aged 81 years.

Who both lived beloved and died lamented.

Also, Mary Harry their daughter, who departed this life the 14th day of March 1796, aged 55 years.

And Moses the son of the above George and Mary Martyn, who departed this life June the 15th 1799, in the 54th year of his age.

In offices of goodness his chief time was spent,
He liv'd a Christian, and he died a Saint.

Also in Memory of Catherine the Daughter of the above said George and Mary Martyn, who departed this life July the 3rd 1803, aged 67 years.

44. Upon an altar tomb :

To the Memory of Elizabeth the wife of George Martyn, Gent., of Newhall in this Parish, and daughter of Edward and Elizabeth Brendon, of the Parish of Lawhitton, in this County, who departed this Life on the 15th day of March 1817, aged 33 years.

Also, to the Memory of Elizabeth the Daughter of the said George and Elizabeth Martyn, who departed this life on the 5th day of April 1809, aged one year and nine months.

Also, to the memory of the above George Martyn of Helland, in this Parish, who died on the 9th day of March 1835, aged 55 years.

45. Upon an altar tomb:

Sacred to the memory of George Martyn of Trewen in the Parish of Lanteglos by Camelford, who departed this life the 8th day of June 1845, aged 29 years.

Also, in memory of Elizabeth Kate, only Daughter of the above George Martyn, who died at Benbole, in the Parish of St Kew, the 2nd of December 1859, aged 16 years.

46. On the base of a Latin cross :

William Martyn, who died July 1870, aged 51.

Also, William his second son, died October 10th 1864, aged 12.

47. Upon an altar tomb :

Sacred to the memory of John Martyn late of Trecarne in the Parish of Tintagel, who departed this life on the 28th July 1855, aged 73 years.

Also, to the Memory of Martha Melluish Martyn, wife of the above, who departed this life on the 24th April, 1855, aged 62 years.

Also, of George their Son who Departed this life on the 6th Sept. 1851, aged 20 years.

Also, of Thomas Henry their Son, who died at Port Elizabeth, South Africa, on the 16th of Feby 1852, aged 37 years.

49. Upon an altar tomb:
Sacred to the memory of Joseph son of John and Martha Martyn of Trecarne, in the Parish of Tintagel, who departed this life on the 30th March 1833, aged one year and nine months.

Also, in Memory of Patty, their Daughter. She departed this life October the 27th 1833, aged four months.

Also, Joseph, their Son, who died of fever at sea and his body committed to the deep near the Island of St. Domingo, on the 10th day of May, A.D. 1841, in the 18th year of his age.

50. Upon an altar tomb:
In Memory of Thomas Wakeham, youngest son of Emanuel and Jane Wakeham, late of Delabole Barton, in this Parish, who died at Camelford July the 19th 1865, aged 58 years.

51. Upon an altar tomb:
Sacred to the Memory of Emanuel Wakeham, Yeoman, late of Tregardock in this Parish, who departed this life on the 28th June 1848, aged 86 years.

Also, Jane wife of the above named Emanuel Wakeham, who departed this life on the first of March 1810, aged 41 years.

Likewise Mary Harry, sister of the aforesaid Jane Wakeham, who departed this life on the 24th Jany 1810, aged 44 years.

THE NEW CEMETERY.

The old Churchyard having become full a piece of land containing more than half an acre, situate on the west side of the Churchyard, was purchased by the parishioners of the Honble Geo. M. Fortescue, at a cost of £150, as an additional burying ground, for which purpose it was consecrated on 18th March 1869.

PARISH REGISTERS.

The old Registers of this parish consist of three volumes, the whole being in pretty good condition.—

Vol. I. This volume contains the record of baptisms, marriages, and burials. The entries commence in 1558, and continue to 1722. It is, from the beginning to 1603, a transcript, under Canon 70, from earlier records, which are not now in existence.

Vol. II contains the entries of baptisms, marriages, and burials, from the former date until 1812.

Vol. III contains the entries of marriages from 1754 to 1812, notwithstanding that they are recorded also in Vol. II.

The earliest names occurring in the registers are : Illary, Andrew, Hockyn, Niccoll, Carveth, Lynham, Trehanneck, Pollard, Hoskyn, Worthivale, Mathew, Taverner, Hender, Phillip, Dagge, Hamley, Penkevell, Belorne, Petigrew, Cocke, Cowlyn, Gilbarte, Chappell, Polgreye, and Cradock.

There is also an old book of Churchwardens' Accounts extending from 1768 to 1834.

CHURCH GOODS.

In the return of Plate and Bells in each Church in the Hundred of Trigg in 1552, it is stated that "the parishioners of St. Etha have one chalice, parcel gilt, and three bells, in the tower there.[1] Of the possessions of the Church some half a century later we find the following Terrier in the Diocesan Registry.—

"DEANERY OF TRIGG MINOR.

St. Tethe. A note of all such Implements wch we, Andrew Marten & John Pollard, wardens for this yere, received of the old wardens for the laste yere, the first day of May 1607.

Imprimis—One Byble of the largest volume, one Communion booke, one paraphrase, one of Mr. Hardins workes, one booke of Cannons, another called the popish imposture in casting out of devils, two little bookes of prayers for the Kinges Matie., Jewell's workes, a booke of Homelyes & 4 other little bookes, & the Register booke, a coveringe for the Pulpitt, a covering for the Communion table, and one table cloth, & a font cloth, with a covering of Tymber, one Communion Cup of silver & a silver cover, two quartes, a pint, a tun, & a little hottell of Gynne!"

It is singular that in the remarkable collection of books the Church did not possess a copy of the Book of Common Prayer; and the necessaries for the decent celebration of Divine Service were very scant indeed. Scarcely any improvement in the last particular is shewn by the Terrier of 1727, in which it is said that: "The utensils of the Church "are four Bells. A broad cloth carpet and white linen cloth and a napkin for the

---

[1] Augmentation Office, Church Goods $\frac{1}{51}$ 6th Edward VI.

" Communion Table, one silver Chalice, a pewter flagon, patten, & Bason for collecting
" the offerings." The Chalice mentioned in the last Terrier is doubtless that now in use,
which bears the date 1661, and the Hall mark of that year.   Maker's mark, D.R.
within a margin, composed of a lozenge within a quatrefoil.

The other utensils for the altar are: an old pewter bason and plate, perhaps the
same mentioned in the last terrier, but the pewter flagon is lost.

SCHOOLS.

In the village, in a large room, part of the old workhouse, a school is kept in which
about sixty of the sons of farmers, &c., are educated; and there are various Dame Schools
within the parish, in which instruction is afforded to about 180 other children; and 108
are educated in a British and Foreign School at Pengelly, which is under Government
Inspection.   A new Board School, for the education of 340 boys, girls, and infants,
designed by Mr. Sylvanus Trevail of St. Blazey, Architect, is about to be erected at
Delabole, and another Board School will be provided at Church Town, designed by the
same architect, for 165 children, upon the mixed system, and infants.   These schools are
for the united parishes of St. Teath and Michaelstow.   In addition to the existing daily
schools, abovementioned, a Sunday School is held in the Church, and also in some of the
Dissenters' Meeting Houses, which are attended by about 120 children.

There are no charitable foundations.

THE MANOR OF DELIOMURE.

The manor of Deliomure (Great Delio) appears in Domesday among the possessions
of the Earl of Moreton, under whom it was held by one Blohinus.   " The Earl holds
one mansion which is called Deliomur, which was held by Jaulus on the day on which
King Edward was alive and dead.   In it is half a hide and it pays gild for one
virgate.   This two ploughs can plow.   This is held by Blohinus of the Earl.   There
Blohinus has one acre and half and one plough in demesne, and the villans have the
rest of the land and one plough.   There Blohinus has eleven villans, and four bordars,
and one bondman, and 4 unbroken mares, and eleven animals, and five pigs, and 15

sheep; one acre of meadow and 20 acres of pasture, and the value per annum is 20s., and when the Earl received it the value was 30 shillings."[1]

According to the Return made to the Justices Itinerant in 12th Edward I. (1284) Deliomure contained nine acres Cornish[2].

Blohinus was the ancester of the family of Bloihou, or Bloyou, by whom the Fee of the manor of the Deliomur was subsequently held. Alan Blohihoie paid scutage for seven knights' fees in Cornwall in 1187,[3] and in 1234, Ralph Blowo was assessed upon seven fees in Polrode, in which Deliomure was included.[4] In 1306, Alan Bloighou died seized, inter alia, of one fee in Delyamur and Niwall (Newhall) of the value of seventy shillings.[5] According to an Inquisition taken at Lostwithiel 1303, Henry Cavell held in Deliomure one fee of Polrode, and at the same time Alan Bloyou is shewn to hold in Polrode and Dennant two fees.[6] In 1346, Roger son of the aforesaid Henry held this fee,[7] and in 1427 it had devolved upon Robert Cavell, Reginald Langford, Roger Prideaux, Thomas Weryng, William Tregartha, John Nicoll, John Tynten, and the heirs of William Bere, who held it separately between them, and because neither of them held a quarter part of a knight's fee, it was not assessable to the aid then levied.[8]

In 1304, the Tything of Deliomure was amerced in the then large sum of 10s. 6d. for default.[9]

The *manor* would seem to have become dismembered at an early period. In 1601, Humphry Nicoll of Penvose died seized of land in Deliomere as portion of the manor of St. Tudy, which had been settled upon him and Jane his wife, in tail male, by a fine levied in Hilary term 12th Elizabeth,[10] and Delymere down belonged to William Cavell of St. Kew.[11]

In 1651, a lease of Langford's Dellamere was granted by William Langford to John Hamley.

In the latter part of the last century several of the tenements were vested in the family of Martyn. By Indentures of lease and release, dated 11th and 12th October 1793, between George Martyn of Helland, in St. Teath, of the one part, and John Martyn of St. Teath of the other part, after reciting that George Martyn was seized in fee simple of Phillipp's Delymure, Langford's Delymure and Inche's Delymure, parcels

---

[1] Exon Domesday, Vol. iv, p. 242, original fo. 263.

[2] Carew's Survey of Cornwall, 1769, p. 47 b.   [3] Pipe Roll, 33rd Henry II.

[4] Testa de Nevill, p. 200. See Hist. of Trigg, Vol. ii, p. 530 and 530 n.

[5] Inq. p.m., 34th Edward I, No. 44.

[6] Original Inquisitions taken upon Fees in co. Cornwall, 31st Edward 1, Sub. Rolls, $\frac{87}{4}$

[7] Book of Aids.

[8] Transcripts of Inquisitions taken for the purpose of levying a Subsidy, 6th Henry VI.

[9] Ministers' Accounts. Account of Thomas de la Hyde, Sheriff and Seneschal of Cornwall, 33rd Edward I, No. 487.

[10] Inq. p.m. 43rd Elizabeth, No. 128, Humphry Nicoll mar. Jane daughter of Richard Roscarrock of Roscarrock.

[11] See Terrier of 1601, ante p. 101.

R

of Delymere, formerly the lands of Catherine Woolacombe, widow, and Elizabeth Woolacombe, spinster, her daughter, the said tenements are conveyed to the said John Martyn.
John Martyn by his will, dated 12th August 1826, charged Delimure with the payment
of an annuity of £60 a year to his wife, and, subject thereto, devised the estate to
John Martyn son of testator's nephew George Martyn, which John Martyn, by deed
dated 30th December 1868, conveyed it to the Hon. G. M. Fortescue of Boconnoc.

Dagg's Delymere had been attached to the manor of Tregardock, which was acquired
by Mr. Pitt, and passed to Mr. Fortescue by devise from Lady Grenville.[1]

MANOR OF DELIABOLL.

This Manor, like Deliomure, at the time of the Domesday Survey formed parcel of
the possessions of the Earl of Moreton, under whom it was held by Roger. " The
Earl holds one mansion which is called Delio, which was held by Lewinus when King
Edward was alive and dead. In it is one hide of land, and it renders gild for eleven
ferlings. This can be ploughed with four ploughs. In it Roger holds one ferling in
demesne, and one plough; this Roger holds of the Earl, and the villans all the rest of
the land. There Roger has one villan, and six bordars, and one bondman, and five
animals, and 25 sheep, and one acre of meadow, and 40 acres of pasture ; and the
value, per annum, is 11 shillings, and when the Earl received it 30 shillings."[2]

According to the Return made to the Justices Itinerant in 12th Edward I (1284),
Deliobol contained six Cornish acres.[3] In 1302, Delyouboll is mentioned as a tithing,
and was amerced for default.[4]

It appears from an Inquisition taken at Lostwithiel, that in 1303, Robert le
Brun held one Fee in Delyouboll of the fees of the Moreton,[5] which fee, in 1346,
was held by William le Brune.[6] Notwithstanding this the fee in chief would appear to
have been vested in the family of Monthermer. Thomas Monte Hermer died s.p.m.,
leaving a sole daughter and heir, who became the wife of Sir John de Montacute, Chr.,[7]

---

[1] Deeds at Boconnoc.
[2] Exon Domesday, Vol. iv, p. 240, original fo. 231.
[3] Carew's Survey of Cornwall, Edit. 1769, p. 476 b.
[4] Assize Roll, 30th Edward I, m. 57, $\frac{m}{1} \begin{Bmatrix} 1 \\ 21 \end{Bmatrix}$
[5] Original Inquisitions taken upon Fees in co. Cornwall, 31st Edward I, Sub. Roll, $\frac{87}{4}$
[6] Book of Aids, Vol. iii, Exchequer, Queen's Remb. Office. The Aid was 40s. upon each fee. but being
one of the small fees of Morton, Robert le Brun was assessed at 25s. only, but he afterwards paid a further
sum of 15s, making up the full amount. Rot. Pip. 31st Edward I.
[7] See Hist. of Trigg, Vol. ii, pp. 125, 126.

and, *inter alia*, carried to him one fee in Delioboll, Hamet and Tracorm, worth 100s. per annum, but the fee remained to Margaret his relict as of her inheritance. She died in 1394 thereof seized, and it descended to Ralph Earl of Westmorland, upon whose attainder, in 1460, it became forfeited to the crown.[1]   **1333881**

The *manor* of Delioboll was, however, possessed by the family of le Brune.

William le Brune, Chr., by his charter dated at Trecorm on Monday next after the feast of the Conversion of St. Paul, 11th Richard II. (1387-8) granted all his lands, &c., in Trecorm, Hamet, Douenant, *Delioboll, Deliopoleyn, Deliocarlebon,* and Lamelyn, with the rents and services of Johanna, who was the wife of Robert Brune, Roger Styrra, and Richard Toker, of the lands which they held, separately, for their lives, with the reversion of the said lands, and the rents and services of John Trelawny, William Attemore, Thomas Treythyan, and Johanna daughter of William de Trevthanet,[2] of lands which they held separately in the villes of Woluestovne, Hamet, Deliov, and Roos, to Stephen Bant, Richard Seka, Clerk, and Roger de Trenant, to hold to them and their heirs for ever, on condition, however, that they should re-enfeoff the said William le Brune in the said lands, to hold to him and the heirs of his body legitimately begotten, in default of such issue to the use of William Brune, bastard, son of the said William Brune, Chr., and the heirs of his body legitimately begotten, and in default of such issue to the right heirs of the said William Brune, Chr. These Charters, however, were never completely executed, and after the death of William le Brune, Chr., Alice Crewen, as sister and one of the heirs of the said William Brune, and Reginald Dallyng, as kinsman and the other heir of the said William: viz., as the son of Johanna another sister of the said William, entered into possession of the said lands. The said Alice had issue a certain Stephen Crewen, who had issue Johanna, who became the wife of Stephen Bodulgate. Reginald Dallyng by his charter, dated at Trecorme on Monday next before the feast of All Saints, 1st Henry IV (1399), granted to the said Stephen Bodulgate and Johanna his wife, his proparty of the said lands: viz., the manors of Delioboll, Trecorme, Hamet, and Lamelyn, to hold to the said Stephen and Johanna and the heirs of their bodies for ever, paying to the said Reginald for the term of his life a rent of four marks per annum, and after the death of the said Reginald to hold of the chief Lord of the fee by the rents and services due and accustomed: in the event, however, of the said Stephen and Johanna dying without heirs of their bodies, all the proparty of the said Reginald in the said manors to revert to his right heirs.[3] Soon after this Thomas Colyn, Robert Colyn son of Margaret

---

[1] See Hist. of Trigg, Vol. ii, p. 125.

[2] It appears from an Inquisition taken at Camelford on Saturday next after the feast of Pentecost, 6th Henry VI (1428), for the purpose of assessing an aid, that Stephen Bodulgate held a quarter part of one fee in Delioboll, and he was assessed to pay 20d. to the aid; and that John Trelauny, Richard at More, Thomas Trethian and Walter Bodulgate held separately between them three parts of the same fee, which had been before held by William le Brune, but as neither of them held a quarter part of a fee they were not assessed to this aid. (Transcripts of Inquisitions 6th Henry VI.)

[3] In 1509, a fine was levied in which Richard Resprenna and Walter Bodulgate were querists, and Stephen Bodulgate and Johanna his wife deforc., by which various lands, *inter alia*, Trecorme, Hamet, Dovnant,

R 2

Treythyan, *alias* Robert Brune, forcibly disseized the aforesaid Stephen Bodulgate and Johanna his wife of their manor of Delioboll, and at the Assizes held at Launceston on Monday next after the feast of St. Lawrence 1406, an assize of view of recognizance was held to inquire if the said disseizing were unjust. Robert Colyn, son of Margaret Trethyan, *alias* Robert Brune, in these proceedings is shewn to have been the son and heir of William Brune, bastard, and to be then aged nine years, but the jury could not come to any conclusion as to whether the disseizing were unjust or no, and left it to the opinion of the judge; but, in respect to the disseizin, they awarded damages to Stephen Bodulgate and Johanna his wife, and found that the said land was not then worth anything beyond the reprises, the said Stephen Bodulgate having granted an annual rent of £20 out of it to Walter Bodulgate his brother.[1]

We have not traced any judgment upon the point of issue, but it appears that in 1425, a precept was issued to the Sheriff (William Talbot) to summon a jury, and by inquisition to inquire if the said Stephen Bodulgate and Johanna his wife had been unjustly disseized by Robert son of Margaret Treythyan, and the Sheriff was commanded, if he found such to have been the case, to imprison the said Robert and Thomas, and give re-seizin to the said Stephen and Johanna, and also damages out of the lands of the said Robert and Thomas according to the statute of re-disseizin. And in 1442, Thomas Talbot, son and heir of the aforesaid William Talbot late Sheriff of Cornwall, was summoned to answer for the late Sheriff as to the bodies of the said Robert and Thomas whom he had taken and imprisoned. Thomas Talbot appeared and said he ought not to be called upon to answer for the said bodies because, he said, no writ was delivered to the said William Talbot, which he was prepared to prove. Nevertheless he was fined 13s. 4d.[2]

Stephen Bodulgate kept possession of the lands, and was seized of them in his demesne as of fee, and, being so seized, enfeoffed John Ward, Clerk, Richard Talvargh and others in, *inter alia*, the manor of Deliowboll, to hold to the use of the said Stephen and his heirs for the fulfilment of his last will. He had issue a son Thomas, and died, and afterwards the said Thomas died, and in 1472 the said John Ward, and Richard Talvargh, the other trustees having died, continued seized of the premises because the will of the said Stephen had not then been fulfilled. The officers of the crown, however, under the colour of certain offences supposed to have been committed by the said Thomas Bodulgate against the King's Majesty, claimed, on the king's behalf, a certain interest in the manors and lands of the said Thomas, as well as the annulment of the will of the aforesaid Stephen, and the disinheriting of the heirs of the said Thomas, who had never transgressed against the King. Accordingly the king

---

Delioboll, and Deliopollen, were settled upon the said Stephen and Johanna his wife and the heirs of their bodies, and in default of such issue remainder to the right heirs of the said Johanna. (Pedes Finium, 11th Henry IV, Michs.)

[1] Assize Rolls, Divers Counties, 7th Henry IV, 2 N/37 {4, m. 86.

[2] Lord Treasurer's Remb. of the Exchequer, 25th Henry VI, Easter, m. 15.

being desirous of doing justice, by Letters Patent dated 18th March 1472-3, remitted to the aforesaid John Ward and Richard Talvargh, and also to Joan Coryton and Isabella Roscarrock, sisters and heirs of the aforesaid Thomas, son and heir of the aforesaid Stephen, all his right and title to the said manors and lands, and also granted that the said Thomas Bodulgate should not be impeached in Parliament, or elsewhere, in respect to any thing which he had done.[1]

In the partition of the Bodulgate estates the manor of Delioboll fell to the share of Isabella, the younger sister of Thomas Bodulgate, who married Thomas Roscarrock.[2] By her charter, dated 15th December 21st Edward IV (1481), she granted, *inter alia*, her messuage in Dyllyoweboll to her son John Roscarrock, to hold to him and his heirs and assigns for ever; and upon her death, in 1488, it was found that the said messuage was held of the Lord Hungerford.[3] John Roscarrock died seized, *inter alia*, of the manor of Deliowboll, 26th October 1537, at which time this manor is said to have been held of the Prince as of his manor of Helston in Trigg.[4]

Delioboll continued in the family of Roscarrock for a considerable time. In 1569 the lands would appear to have been annexed to the reputed manor of Bodulgate, and were then held by Humphry Roscarrock and Nicholas Roscarrock.[5] Nevertheless, Richard Roscarrock died seized, *inter alia*, of the Manor of Delioboll in 1575, leaving Thomas Roscarrock his son and heir,[6] who died seized, *inter alia*, of this manor on 2nd February 1586-7, it then being held, with Bodulgate, of the manor of Helston in Trigg, and John Roscarrock was found to be his son and heir.[7] In 1586 John Roscarrock, Esq., and Catherine his wife, suffered a fine to Charles Trevanion, Esq., in one messuage, one garden, one orchard, 120 acres of land, sixty acres of meadow, sixty acres of pasture, 120 acres of furze and heath, and twenty acres of moor in Deleboll, alias Deleoboll, and St. Teath, and quitclaimed the same to the said Charles for ever.[8] A few years ago Mr. Trevanion of Caerhayes sold his estate therein to the " Delabol Slate Company."

[1] The original Patent is at Coker Court, co. Somerset. (See Hist. of Trigg, Vol. ii, p. 362).
[2] See Pedigree of Roscarrock, Hist. of Trigg, vol. i, p. 562.   [3] Inquis. p.m. 3rd Henry VI, No. 117.
[4] Inq. p. m. 28th and 29th Henry VIII. Escheator's Inquisitions, see Hist. of Trigg, Vol. ii, p. 341.
[5] See Hist. of Trigg, Vol. ii, 345.
[6] Inq. p.m. Wards and Liveries, 18th, 19th, 20th Elizabeth, Vol. xviij, p. 33.
[7] Inq. p.m. 30th Elizabeth, Part i, No. 82.
[8] Ped. Fin. 38th Elizabeth, Trinity.

DELABOLE (DELIOBOLI) SLATE QUARRIES.

These celebrated quarries have been worked, to a greater or less extent, for a considerable period.   The slate raised here is of very good quality, of a blue colour, light and durable.   It is considered the best produced in England.[1]   Borlase, writing of this quarry in 1758, says that for its lightness and enduring the weather the slate[2] is greatly preferred to any slate in Great Britain ; and he describes the quarry as being 300 yards long, 100 yards wide, and 40 fathoms (or 240 feet) deep ; adding that " all the slate is carried with no small danger on men's backs, which are guarded from the weight by a kind of leathern apron or cushion."   The pit is now rather of an eliptical form, and measures about 450 yards by 200 yards, and its average depth, where it is still worked, is about 300 feet ; its greatest depth 400 feet, so that it is not much deeper than when Borlase wrote.   Much of the debris is thrown into the exhausted parts of the quarry ; nevertheless there are hills of rubble surrounding the quarry some 200 feet high, which may be seen from a considerable distance, and cover an area of ninety acres.

The strata of slate run north and south, the beds dipping from east to west about three inches in the foot, with a slight fall from north to south.   The lamination is not produced by the bedding, but is due to a metamorphism called " cleavage," which often traverses the rock at right angles to the lines of stratification, and in the Delabole quarries is nearly horizontal.   Hence the method of excavation, or working the quarry, differs from that practised in Wales, where the cleavage is nearly perpendicular, and the quarries are worked in galleries, and not, as at Delioboll, in pits.

The slates produced receive peculiar technical names, according to their sizes :
Queens are 36, 34, and 32 inches by 18, 17, and 16 inches.
Princesses 30, 28, and 26 inches by 15, 14. and 13 inches.
Duchesses 24 inches by 12 inches.
Marchionesses 22 inches by 11 inches.
Countesses 20 inches by 10 inches.
Viscountesses 18 inches by 9 inches.
Ladies 16 inches by 8 inches.
Small Ladies 14 inches by 7 inches.
Doubles 12 inches by 6 inches.
In addition to these, which are called " size slate," there is a large rough kind of

---

[1] Carew, writing of the Cornish slate at the end of the 16th century, probably of that of this quarry, says : it " is in substance thinne, in colour faire, in waight light, in lasting strong, and generally carrieth so good regard, as (besides the supply for home prouision) great store is yeerely conueied by shipping both to other parts of the Realme, and also beyond the Seas into Britaine and Netherland." (Survey of Cornwall, p. 6.)

[2] Natural History of Cornwall, Oxford, 1758, p. 94.

varying dimensions, having one side uncut, called, from their ragged appearance when piled in the yard, "rags." Also there is a small irregular kind called "scantle," made of pieces too small to cut "size slate" from. Besides the various sizes of roofing slate, there is a large production of flagstones, or slabs, cut from large stones, or stones too coarse for thin cleavage. These are exceedingly durable, not only when exposed to atmospheric influence with inscriptions (as on tombstones) upon them, but for pavements, and not only internally but externally also, as the stones are not liable to be damaged by frost. They are also used to a considerable extent for making water cisterns, troughs, &c., for which they are highly esteemed for their durability and lightness, and are in great demand for all purposes. Moreover, they are often used, polished, for mantel pieces and other interior ornamental purposes.

In the early part of the present century these quarries were worked by various proprietors, among the principal of whom was Mr. Robert Bake, who employed about forty men. The method of working was of a very primitive character, there being no machinery except of the simplest kind. The product, beyond what was required for home consumption, was conveyed to Port Isaac, a distance of six miles, in wagons drawn by six oxen led by one horse. Mr. Bake kept two such teams. When a sufficient quantity had accumulated at the Port it was shipped, frequently for France. After Mr. Bake's death in 1810, the quarry was leased, and afterwards purchased by Mr. T. R. Avery of Boscastle, who by his vigorous energy greatly extended the works. He afterwards leased it to Messrs. Grainger and Trickett of Plymouth, who erected the first steam engine. Finding their capital too small to carry on the work with advantage they assigned their lease of the quarry called Leaseworth in 1871 to the "Old Delabol Slate Company" (the present Company,) to whom Mr. Avery afterwards sold the land, continuing to work an adjoining pit called Landwork, the property of Mr. Hocken. Soon afterwards his lease expired, when those quarries passed into the hands of the "Old Delabol Slate Company," and not long after this Mr. Avery sold to the Company the land of Leaseworth. In 1844 the Company rented and subsequently purchased the estate of Mr. Trevanion of Caerhayes in Delabole. On the expiration of Mr. Avery's lease in Landwork the Company took it for a term of fourteen years, but in 1864 they purchased the fee and are now the sole proprietors of the whole of the Delabole quarries. They have introduced all necessary machinery and appliances for the proper prosecution of the work. In 1871 there were employed in these quarries 450 men and 130 boys, who worked chiefly by timework, and about 1200 tons of slate and rubbish were daily raised, whilst 16,000 tons of slate were annually shipped at Port Gavern, whither it was conveyed in wagons by the neighbouring farmers.

MANOR OF DELIONEWITH *alias* DELIONEWTH.

It appears from certain proceedings in the courts of law between 1337-90, that the manor of Delyonnewy'th, *inter alia*, belonged to the family of Tredeforde. By her charter, dated at Tredeford on Wednesday next after the feast of St. Faith the Virgin, 43rd Edward III (1369), Johanna de Tredeforde granted the same lands to William Fitz-Water (Walter) whom she married, to hold of her and her heirs to the said William and his heirs of her begotten, at the annual rent of £40, and after her decease to render to her right heirs, annually, one grain of wheat. The said Johanna having died, the said William Fitz-Walter was seized of the said manors and lands according to the terms of the charter, and took to wife a certain Alice, and died on the feast of the Ascension 1385, leaving a son and heir named Thomas, a minor, whose wardship was vested in Henry Ivelcombe, Knt.[1] In January 1386-7, Alice, as the relict of the said Sir William Fitz-Walter, claimed against the said Henry, dower of the lands of her late husband Sir William Fitz-Walter, *inter alia*, of the manors of Tredeford and Delionewyth. The case was then postponed, but came on for judgment before the Justices of Assize at Launceston 1392, before which date the said Alice had intermarried with John Deneys of Gidecote, who was joined with her as plaintiff. The jury was unable to determine whether the said John Deneys and Alice had right of dower in the said lands or no, and petitioned the discretion of the judges, when the trial was postponed.[2]

We have no further account of the manor for a considerable period.

In the early part of the 17th century the manor of Delionuth belonged to the family of Chaple of St. Teath. On the death of Richard Billing of Lanke, in 1624, it was found that he died seized, *inter alia*, of fifty acres of arable, meadow, and pasture land in Delynewth, which he held of John Chaple, Gent., as of his manor of Delynewith in free socage;[3] and upon the marriage of John Chaple the younger, son of the abovementioned John Chaple, with Mary Hardye, daughter of Alice Hardye of Launceston, Widow, by indenture, dated 30th June, 3rd Charles (1627), he settled, *inter alia*, his manor of Delionuth to his own use for life, and remainder to the said John Chaple the younger, and Mary his wife for life, remainder to their issue in tail male, and in default of such issue, remainder to the issue of any daughters of such marriage, and, in default, remainder to the right heirs of the said John Chaple, the younger, for ever.[4]

This manor has long been dismembered.

---

[1] De Banco Rolls, 10th Richard II, Hil. m. 319.　　　[2] De Banco Roll, 14th Richard II, Michs. m. 335.
[3] Inq., p.m. Wards and Liveries, 21st James. Bundle 27.　　　[4] Deed, pencs Colonel Grylls of Lewarne.

MANOR OF NEWHALL.

This manor was anciently parcel of the possessions of the family of Bloyou,[1] being held with the manor of Polrode, under which it frequently passed, and came into the family of Carminow, with the other Bloyou estates. William Carminow, son of Sir Walter Carminow and Alice Tinten, granted it, *inter alia*, to Alice relict of his brother Ralph, for her life in the name of dower. This lady, by her charter dated 17th June 1407, released it, together with the manor of Polrode and others, to John Carminow son and heir of the aforesaid William, for the purpose of securing an annuity of 100 marks per annum to Sir William Bonville, whom she afterwards married, and who died on the feast of St. Valentine following.[2] Whether or no, this manor continued in the possession of the Carminow family until the 17th century we are unable to state, but in 1680 lands in Newhall were held by the Lord Roberts,[3] and the manor of Newhall now forms parcel of the possessions of the present Lord Robartes; but we regret to say that we have been unable to obtain any information as to the manner of its acquisition.

MANOR OF TREWOSELL *alias* TREROOSELL.

– The manor of Trewosell, now called Treroosell, formed parcel of the possessions of the Priory of Launceston, and in the valuation of the lands and tenements of that house is entered as being worth £2 13s. 4d. per annum, but out of it was paid to John Kympthorne, bailiff there, 6s. 8d. per annum.[4] On the dissolution of the priory this manor fell into the hands of the king, who, by letters patent dated 29th March 1546, granted it, together with the manor of Lannoweseynt *alias* St. Kew, and other manors and lands, under the description of "all that Lordship and Manor of Trewosell and Treburtheke," to John Wollacombe, Clerk, and Roger Prideaux, Gent., to hold to them and their heirs for ever by the 40th part of one knight's fee, and a rent for this manor of 7s. 5d. per annum. The issues of the manor were then valued at 74s. 2d. per annum.[5] This purchase was to the use of the said Roger Prideaux. The manor continued in the family of Prideaux for a long period. On 10th February 1548-9

---

[1] It was part of the fee held in Delymure by Alan Bloyou in 1306. Inq. p.m. 34th Edward I, No. 44.

[2] Inq. p.m., 9th Henry IV, No. 42.

[3] See Terrier, dated 10th March 1679-80, ante p. 102.   [4] Oliver's Mon. Exon, p. 27.

[5] Rot. Pat., 37th Henry VIII, Part 7, m. 2.   See also Hist. of Trigg, Vol. i, pp. 143, 144, and Vol. ii, p. 90.

S

Roger Prideaux obtained a license to settle, *inter alia*, the manor of Trewosell with Treburthick upon Philippa Parker, widow,[1] whom he was about to marry, and afterwards espoused.[2] And on 29th December 1563 Roger Prideaux obtained another license to alienate the same manor to his brother, William Prideaux, Gent.[3] William Prideaux died 27th June 1564, and by his will, dated two days previously, devised, *inter alia*, to his wife Jone two parts of the manors of Trewosal and Treburthecke.[4] On 1st April 1615 John Prideaux, Junr., Gent., son and heir apparent of John Prideaux, Senr. (who was son and heir of the abovementioned William and Joan) and Abigail his wife obtained a license to alienate the manors of Trewosell and Treburthicke, &c., also the tithe of the fisheries at Padstow, to Humphry Prideaux, Esq., to hold to the said Humphry and his heirs and assigns for ever;[5] and a fine was levied accordingly, the consideration for which was £200.[6] Humphry Prideaux died the same year seized, *inter alia*, of this manor[7] which devolved upon his eldest son and heir Nicholas Prideaux, who dying in 1653, s.p., also so seized[8] it passed with his other estates to his brother Humphry Prideaux, who left an only daughter and heir, Ann, who married her cousin John Prideaux, third son of Sir Peter Prideaux of Netherton, Bart., to whom she carried this manor. John Prideaux died in 1706, s.p., having by his will, dated 10th July 1703,[9] devised, *inter alia*, his manors and lands to his nephew Peter Prideaux, in tail male, in default to his own brother Peter Prideaux, under a like limitation, in default to his nephew Edmund Prideaux, with the same limitation, and in default to John Prideaux, brother of his nephew Peter, with a like limitation. The former estates having failed, the lands devolved upon the last mentioned John Prideaux, who eventually became the sixth Baronet of Netherton. The manor continued in the Prideaux family for a long period, but would seem to have become dismembered, for on the sale out of Chancery, in 1789, of a portion of the estates of Sir John Prideaux of Netherton, Bart., the Quit or Chief Rents of Trewosal, amounting altogether to £1 1s. 2d. per annum, were included in the sale of the Sheaf Tithe of St. Minver and other property, to the Rev. W. Sandys, and realized the sum of £3,000.[10] It has now descended to Mrs. Stephens of St. Minver House.

In 1558, the manor of Colquite paid a chief rent of 2s. 6d per annum to the Manor of Trewosell.[11]

---

[1] Daughter and heir of Roger Yorke, Serjeant at Lawe. (See Ped Hist. of Trigg, Vol. ii, p. 226).
[2] Rot. Pat., 3rd Edw. VI, Part 2, m. 20.   [3] Rot. Pat., 6th Eliz., Part 2, m. 25,
[4] Will proved at Exon.   Bishop's Peculiars.   [5] Rot. Pat., 13th James, Part 33, No. 39.
[6] Pedes Finium, 13th James, Trinity.   [7] Inq. p.m., 15th James.
[8] Inq. p.m., 19th Charles.   [9] Proved 29th June 1707, P.C.C. (Poley, 149).
[10] See ante p. 14. Chancery— Masters' Reports 1784, letter P, Easter Term.
[11] See Hist. of Trigg, Vol ii, p. 481.

MANOR OF TREGARADOC *alias* TREGRADECK *alias* TREGARDOCK.

This manor appears in Domesday under the name of Tregaraduc. It was one of the manors given by the Conqueror to the Earl of Moreton, and was held of the Earl by Alwardus, who had held it in the time of Edward the Confessor. "The Earl holds one mansion which is called Tragaraduc, which was held by Alwardus on the day on which King Edward was alive and dead. In it there is half a hide, and it pays gild for three ferlings. This three ploughs can plough. This is held by Alwardus of the Earl. There Alwardus has one ferling and half a carucate in demesne, and the villans have the rest of the land, and two ploughs. There Alwardus has four villans, and six bordars, and two bondservants, and fifty sheep, and ten acres of pasture; and the value per annum is 10s., and when the Earl received it 20s."[1]

In 1196 Pharamus de Walebraus held half a knight's fee in Tregaradock, and he suffered a fine therein and in twenty-four marks of chattels to Guy de Wautam, who had married Beatrice the daughter of the said Pharamus, and claimed to hold the said fee and chattels for the term of his life, and the said Pharamus quitclaimed the same to him and his heirs for ever.[2]

In 1303 John son of William (Fitz-William?) held a quarter part of one knight's fee in Tregradet, and at the aid levied on the marriage of the eldest daughter of King Edward I, in 1289, Reginald de Moun held in Tregradek the quarter part of the fee which John the son of William had first held.[3] In 1428 the quarter part of this fee in Tregradoc was held by William Moun, Thomas Moun, John Trevelow, and Thomas Restarrek between them. and because neither of them held a quarter part, it was not chargeable to the aid.[4]

John, son of William, held also half a knight's fee in Amal, and this together with Tregradoc, descended to the Mohuns. Reginald de Mohun, in 1347, recovered, *inter alia*, both these manors after unjust deseizin.[5] Sir William Mohun died seized, *inter alia*, of the same manors on 6th April 1588, leaving his son, Reginald Mohun, his nearest heir.[6] It formed one of the manors sold to Thomas Pitt in 1720, from whom it descended to the Honble. George Mathew Fortescue, of Boconnoc, the present possessor.

C. S. Gilbert mentions that in his time there were at Tregardock the remains of an ancient chapel, the origin of which was unknown, and he adds that a few years previously part of a stone font remained within the walls, and that the adjoining field was then, as it is still, known by the name of Chapel Park. No remains can now be traced.

---

[1] Exon Domesday, Vol. IV, p. 243, orig. fo. 263 b.

[3] Book of Aids, Excheq., Queen's Remb. Office, Vol. iii.

[5] Assize Roll, $\begin{matrix} N \\ 2 \\ 22 \end{matrix}$ 3. m. 3. Vide Hist. of Trigg, Vol. ii, p. 123.

[2] Ped. Fin., 8th Richard I. Michs.

[4] Transcripts of Inq., 6th Henry VI.

[6] Inq., p.m. 30th Elizabeth Part 2, No. 43.

S*

Rental of the Manor of Tregardock 1748. *From the Muniments at Boconnoc*

Tenants	Tenements.	Rent.		
Chief Rents.		£	s.	d.
Clinton, John Lord ... ... } Trevela		0	4	0
Brown, Tenant ... ... }				
Darrel, his heirs... ... ... } Trelya		0	1	0
Same tenement ... ... }				
Eliot. Richard, Esq. ... ... } Trevela		0	4	0
Mr. George Martyn, Tenant }				
Pomery, or his heirs, ... } Trevela		0	8	0
Same tenant ... ... }				
Conventionary Tenants.				
Brown, John ... ... Trevela		1	8	8
Brown, John & George Martyn ... Hayne's Tenement		1	1	0
Brown. John & Thomas Jenkyn ... Cowling's Tenement in Tregragon		0	13	4
Brown, Patience ... ... Trelega		0	11	0
Garrow, Robert ... ... Dagg's Delameer		1	4	0
Hocking, Mr. William ... ... Noon's Park		1	8	8
Kent, Grace, Widow ... ... Tregragon, Stephens's Tenement		0	14	4
Libby, Simon ... ... Johnson's Tenement in Trelega		0	11	0
Martyn, Mr. George . ... Noon's Park		1	8	8
Phillips, Mrs. Gertrude ... ... House Tenement in Tregardock		2	2	0
Ditto ... ... Hocken's Tenement in Tregardock		1	1	0
Phillips, Mr. Jonathan ... ... Wester Terreby		0	17	8
Ditto ... ... Easter . Ditto		0	17	8
Watts, William ... ... Brown's Tenement		2	2	0
Ditto ... ... Tubb's Tenement		1	1	0
Ditto ... ... Prade Park		0	6	0
	Total ...	£17	17	0[1]

MANOR OF TREHANNICK.

This manor was taxed in Domesday under the name of Trehynoc, and was held by Reginald of the Earl of Moreton. "The Earl has one mansion which is called Trehynoc, which Algar held on the day on which King Edward was alive and dead. In it is one virgate of land and it renders gild for one acre. This can be ploughed with one plough. Reginald holds this of the Earl. There Reginald has two ferlings in demesne and one plough, and the villans two ferlings. There Reginald has two villans, and two bordars,

[1] There is an error in the cast.

and one bondman, and two cows, and 20 sheep, and the value per annum is 10s., and when the Earl received it the value was the same."[1] According to the Return of 12th Edward I (1284) the fee of Trehanek contained nine Cornish acres.[2] In 1303, Mathew and Agnes Trehonet held in Trehonet half a fee of the fees of Moreton.[3] In 1346, John Trehaurek was returned as holding half a small fee in Treonek, which Mathew and Agnes Treonek had previously held. This he must have held of Sir John Dauny as Lord Paramount, for the said Sir John Dauny on 3rd August in this year died seized, *inter alia*, of one knight's fee in Trehanek and Pendrym, which was of the value of 40d. per annum, and Emelina his daughter was found to be his nearest heir.[4]

In 1427, Robert Cavell, Benedict Trehanek, Richard Pentyr, John Trewynam, Nicholas Watte, Stephen Tregartha and John Leta, held separately between them the moiety of a small fee in Trehanek, which John Trehauerek sometime held, and as neither of them held a quarter part of one fee it was not assessed.[5]

That the manor of Trehannek was for a considerable period held by a family of the same name would seem to be more than probable, though we have only inferential evidence from collateral circumstances.

In 1262, William de Dennant and Isabella his wife, and John de Trehonet and Katherine his wife suffered a fine to Stephen de Carkyan of one messuage, &c., in Trebonet, whereby the said messuage was quitclaimed to the said William and his heirs for ever, to be held of the said William and Isabella and John and Katherine and their heirs at the annual rent of one clove for all services.[6]

A small meadow and then afterwards the stream which supplied the mill were held of the Duchy of Cornwall as of the Manor of Helston in Trigg. In 1337 among the free tenants of the manor were Nicholas Trehonek and Johanna Trehaverock, who held a small meadow in Trehanek for which the said Johanna did fealty.[7] In 1469 Nicholas Trehanek, cousin and heir of Nicholas Trehanek and Johanna Trehaverock, paid a chief rent of 4d. per annum for the bed of a mill in Trehanek.[8] In 1491 it would seem to have been held by another Nicholas Trehanek, probably the son of the last mentioned Nicholas,[9] and he continued to hold it at the following assession.[10] In 1539 John Trehanek, son and heir of Nicholas and Johanna Trehanek, held it.[11] In 1553 it had passed to Johanna, Margery, and Dorothy, daughters and heirs of Thomas Trehanek, which Thomas was the son and heir of John Trehanek, who took it at the previous assession.[12] In 1567 the properties of the said Margery and Dorothy in this

---

[1] Exon Domesday, Vol. iv, p. 236, original fo. 256 b.
[2] Carew's Survey of Cornwall, p. 7 d.
[3] Original Inquisitions taken upon Fees, 31st Edward I.   Subsidy Roll, $\frac{87}{4}$
[4] Inquisition p.m., 20th Edward III, No. 33. (1st Nos.)
[5] Transcripts of Inquisitions taken for the purpose of levying a Subsidy, 6th Henry VI.
[6] Pedes Finium, 46th Henry III, Michaelmas.
[7] Caption of Seizin, Edward the Black Prince.   [8] Assession Roll, 9th Edw. IV.
[9] Ibid. 7th Henry VII.   [10] Ibid. 13th Henry VII.
[11] Ibid. 31st Henry VIII.   [12] Ibid. 1st Mary.

mill bed were held, by reason of purchase, by Ralph Mychell, and the other proparty was held by John Bright in right of Johanna his wife, the other daughter and heir of the aforesaid Thomas Trehanek.[1] In 1574 it was held by the aforesaid Ralph Mitchell and Thomas Kelliou in right of Alice his wife, daughter and heir of Johanna, late wife of John Bright.[2] Ten years later Thomas Kylleowe, Senr., and Thomas Kylleowe, Junr., and Florence his wife, suffered a fine to Richard Mychell, Gent., of one messuage, one corn mill, six gardens, 20 acres of land, 14 acres of meadow, 40 acres of pasture, six acres of furze and heath, and three acres of wood in Trehanek and Trehaneke mill.[3] Richard Mychell would now seem to have become the possessor of the entirety.

The *manor* of Trehannick would appear to have become dismembered as early as in 1533, for in that year Henry Nycoll of Penvose held lands, *inter alia*, in Trehanet, and suffered a fine therein, by which the said lands were settled upon him for life, remainder to John Nycoll his son, and the heirs of the said John.[4] Trehannick would then appear to be parcel of the manor of St. Tudy, and in January 1569-70, Humphry Nycoll, Esq., suffered a fine in the said manor of St. Tudy, of which, *inter alia*, Trehanek and Delymur are described as tenements, to Richard Roscarrock, Gent., by which the said manor and tenements were settled upon the said Humphry and Jane his wife, and the heirs of their bodies, in default remainder to the right heirs of the said Humphry.[5]

In January 1588-9, lands in Trehanecke formed parcel of the manor of Trefreake, and by fine passed from John Chudleigh to Thomas Stone, Esq.[6]

Trehannick soon after the last mentioned date was possessed by Thomas Carminow, who died in 1640, leaving a son, William Carminow, and three daughters. William Carminow died in 1646, leaving by his wife Frances, who subsequently married Phillip Lower, an infant son, William, who, in conjunction with the said Philip Lower and Frances his wife, aunt of the said William (who probably had dower in the lands,) Blanche Mitchel, widow, and Edmund Arundell, Gent., who had married Jane, another aunt of the said William, in 1667, suffered a fine in one messuage, two water grain mills, &c., in St. Teath to Sir James Smith, Knt.,[7] This we conceive must have been Trehannick, for, in 1678, we find Sir James Smith described as of Trehannick.[8] Sir James Smith died soon after this, and Trehannick passed to the family of Beale. William Beale of Trewinnall, by his will, dated 1st May 1712,[9] devised to his son Mathew Beale, subject to an annuity of £10 to testator's wife Juliana, all his lands called Trehannock, Trehannock Mills, &c., in St. Teath, together with the Prebend, Sheaf, Rectory, Impropriation, and Chancel of the parish Church of St. Teath, to hold to him and his heirs in tail male, in default remainder to other sons of testator under similar limitations, and in default remainder over to his daughter Dorothy, to which Dorothy he devised five closes of land, part of the said Barton. In 1715, a recovery was passed in which Thomas Martin, Esq.,

[1] Assession Roll, 9th Elizab.   [2] Ibid. 16th Elizab.
[3] Ped. Finium, 25th and 26th Elizab. Michs.   [4] Pedes Finium, 25th Henry VIII, Trinity.
[5] Pedes Finium, 12th Elizabeth, Hilary.   [6] Ibid, 31st Elizabeth, Hilary.
[7] Pedes Finium 19th Charles II, Michaelmas. See pedigree of CARMINOW, post.
[8] See Hist. of Trigg, Vol. ii, p. 337. See also ibid, 324, n.
[9] Probate 22nd March 1713-4, Archdeaconry of Cornwall.

was petitioner, and Joseph Scott, defendant, in which Matthew Beale, was called to warrant three messuages, two water corn mills, common of turbary, fishery, free warren, and royalties, &c., in Trehannick, also the Prebend, &c., of St. Teath.[1] This was doubtless for purposes of settlement, for we find that Matthew Beale, Esq., held the mill bed aforesaid of the manor of Helston in 1717, as did his heirs in 1731,[2] he having died in 1727.

Very soon after this we find the property vested in Samuel Lyne of Launceston, Gent., who, by his will, dated 5th February 1735, after several pecuniary legacies, devised all his real, and the residue of his personal estate to certain trustees, after the payment of his debts, &c., to the sole use of his grandaughters and coheirs, Elizabeth, Joanna, and Penelope Cheyne, daughters of Edmund Cheyne of Launceston, Esq., and he appointed the said trustees his executors in trust. The trustees having renounced the executorship, adminstration was granted, on 6th September 1737, to Edmund Cheyne until one of his daughters should attain full age. The coheirs subsequently agreed to partition the estate, in which partition, under indentures dated 9th September 1745, the portion which contained, *inter alia*, the barton of Trehanneck and the great tithes of the parish of St. Teath, fell to the share of Elizabeth Cheyne the eldest coheir. Elizabeth Cheyne afterwards married George Fursdon of Fursdon, co. Devon, Esq., and by the marriage settlement, dated 23rd and 24th November 1753, in consideration of a competent settlement made upon her, chargeable upon the lands of inheritance of the said George Fursdon, *inter alia*, the Barton of Trehanneck was conveyed by the said Elizabeth Cheyne, with the concurrence of her sisters Johanna Cheyne, then the wife of John Sawle, Esq., and Penelope Cheyne, to the use of the said George Fursdon, his heirs and assigns for ever, which was confirmed by an indenture dated 28th April 1759, and by a fine the same year.[3] George Fursdon, by his will, dated 6th January 1771, devised to certain trustees, *inter alia*, all his messuages, &c., called Trehanneck and Trehanneck Mills, to hold to the use of his daughter Elizabeth Penelope Fursdon in fee tail, which estate was, by indenture, dated 9th and 10th June 1786, and a common recovery suffered in Trinity Term, 26th George III, converted into a fee simple estate in favour of the said Penelope Fursdon, who immediately afterwards married John Lyon of the city of Exeter, Esq., and by settlement thereupon made, the barton of Trehanneck, together with the mills thereto belonging, were, *inter alia*, conveyed to Francis Coleman, Robert Cooper Lee, Esq., and others, under certain trusts therein named, with power of sale with the consent and approbation of the aforesaid John and Elizabeth Penelope Fursdon, or the survivor of them. In exercise of this power of sale Francis Coleman, as sole surviving trustee of the settlement, with the concurrence of the said John Lyon, the husband (his wife being then dead), by Indentures of lease and release, dated 14th and 15th June 1798, sold to Nicholas Male of St. Teath, Gentleman, who had for some years been in occupation of the estate, all the aforesaid premises, together with the great, or sheaf, tithe arising therefrom, to hold to the said Nicholas Male his heirs and assigns for ever. Nicholas Male

[1] Recoveries, 1st George, Trinity, m. 117.   [2] Assession Rolls, 1717, 1731.
[3] Pedes Finium, 1759, Trinity

made his will on 11th September 1815, and by a codicil thereto, dated 6th October 1815,[1] devised the said premises to his son, Nicholas Male, in fee.   By Declaration of the said Nicholas Male, dated 11th November, and confirmed by the Tithe Commissioners on 16th November 1839, the sheaf tithes arising from the said premises were merged in the freehold.   The said Nicholas Male died in 1871, when the barton of Trehannick and Trehannick Mills, *inter alia*, devolved upon his son Nicholas Male of Camelford, Gent., the present proprietor.

MANOR OF DAUNAND, *alias* DAUNANT, *alias* DANNONDOSSEL.

The name of this manor has been written in a great variety of forms as, Dawnant, Deunand, Dawnath, Dawnauth, Dannon, Dannondossel. Dannon Chapel, &c.   It appears in Domesday under the form of Dvvenant, when it was held by Blohui of the Earl of Moreton, in succession to Alward, who was the possessor in the time of King Edward the Confessor.   "The Earl has one mansion which is called Duuenant, which was held by Alward on the day on which King Edward was alive and dead.   In it is half a hide and it pays gild for one virgate.   This three ploughs can plough.   Blohui holds it of the Earl. There Blohui has one ferling and one carucate and half in demesne, and the villan has the rest of the land.   There Blohui has one villan, and three bond servants, and three animals, and three pigs, and 50 sheep, and 20 she goats, and 40 acres of pasture, and the value per annum is 15 shillings, and when the Earl received it 25s."[2]

This Blohui, elsewhere called Blohinus, who held also the manor of Delio (Deliomure) was, as we have already seen, the ancestor of the family of Bloyou.[3]   Alan Blohunt held seven knight's fees in Cornwall, 33rd Henry II,[4] and in 31st Edward I, another Alan held in Polroda and in Dounant two fees.[5]   In 20th Edward 3rd (1346) these two fees were held by Alice Carminow,[6] and in 6th Henry VI (1428) the two fees in Polrode and Davnant which Alice[7] Carmynow formerly held were held by Thomas Carmynow,

---

[1] Proved Archd. Court of Cornwall, 11th November 1817.

[2] Exon Domesday, Vol. iv, p. 243.

[3] On the death of Edmund Earl of Cornwall, it was found that of the 121 knights' fees which he held in Cornwall, Ralph Bloyou held in Polrode six fees of the value of £30, each fee being of the value of 100s.. Inq., p.m., 28th Edward I, No. 44.

[4] Red Book of the Exchequer, fo. 59 *d*.

[5] Original Inquisitions, 31st Edward I, Subsidy Roll, $\frac{87}{4}$

[6] Book of Aids Exchequer, Queen's Remembrance Office, Vol. iii, 33—36.

[7] Alice was wife of Sir Walter Carminow and daughter and heir of Sir Stephen Tynten by Elizabeth daughter and heir of Alan Bloyou. (See Ped. post.)

Benedict Trehannek, Roger Prideaux, and Robert Escote, separately between them, as for a quarter part of one fee, and by John Wydeslade, John Trecarne, sen., William Tregartha, the heirs of John Carne, and Ralph Botreaux for three parts of one fee; and by John Passeleygh, Stephen Cligh, William Miller, John Hoygge, the heirs of Richard Hewissh, Richard Lamelyn, Richard Belyon, Thomas Rescarrek, and John Gyfford as for a moiety of another fee. The other moiety would seem to have been lost. And because neither of them held a full quarter part of one fee they were not assessable under the act.[1]

In the Return of Cornish acres, 12th Edward I, Polroda is rated at fifteen acres, in which is included Dounant.[2]

The *manor* of Dawnant anciently formed parcel of the possessions of the family of Peverell, and descended, in like manner as Hamatethy and Park, to the two daughters and heirs of Sir Thomas Peverell.[3] In the Inquisition post mortem of Margaret Peverell, relict of the said Sir Thomas, who died 14th August 1422, the manor of Daunand is said to be held of Hugh Courtenay, Knt., Hugh Luttrell, Knt.,[4] John Selman, and John Fortescue, by what service the jury stated they were ignorant, and they say, as to the extent of the manor, that it consisted of one carucate of land of the clear yearly value of 13s. 4d., of two acres of meadow of the clear yearly value of 12d., of one corn mill of the clear yearly value of 3s. 4d., of twenty acres of wood, the pasture of which was worth yearly 12d., and of 10s. Rents of Assize paid by divers free tenants there.[5] Immediately upon the death of Margaret Peverell, her two daughters settled the estates, *inter alia*, the manor of Daunant, so that it devolved by the death of Alianora, the elder daughter and coheir of the said Margaret, and wife of Sir William Talbot, s.p., upon Robert Hungerford son and heir of Katherine the other daughter and heir of the said Margaret.[6] The manor of Daunant, or Dawnoth, as frequently written, descended with the other Hungerford estates, and suffered the same vicissitudes and forfeitures, as have been described under the manor of Hamatethy.[7] It formed a portion of the re-grant, after surrender, to Sir Walter Hungerford, by letters patent dated 5th July 1558,[8] and by letters patent dated 5th May 1604, the King granted to Edmund Hungerford, son of the said Sir Walter, for the good services he had rendered Queen Elizabeth, all the remainder and reversion, *inter alia*, of the manor of Dawnoth, with appurtenances in Cornwall[9].

[1] Transcripts of Inquisitions, 6th Henry VI.   [2] Carew's Survey, p. 47b.   [3] See Ped., Hist. of Trigg, vol. i, 383.
[4] Sir Hugh Courtenay married Margaret daughter and one of the coheirs of Thomas Carminow, mentioned above in the text, who was grandson of Alice Carminow, who held the fee of Downant in chief in 1346.
[5] Inquisition p.m., 1st Henry VI, No. 43.
[6] It appears from an Inquisition taken 30th September 1474, that Walter Hungerford was seized, *inter alia*, of the manor of Dawnoth, valued at 43s. 4d. per annum, held of the Lord of Carmanton (Carnanton), by the service of 2 lbs. of Gariophili. The Lord of Carnanton, at this date, was Richard, Duke of Gloucester, afterwards King Richard III, who had married the Lady Ann Neville, one of the daughters and coheirs of Richard Nevill, Earl of Warwick. See Hist. of Trigg, Vol. i, p. 31.
[7] Ibid., pp. 357, 362.
[8] Rot. Pat. 4th and 5th Philip and Mary, Part ii, m. 9.   [9] Rot. Pat. 2nd James, Part 25.

This manor, however, would seem to have been divided into moieties in the time of Henry VIII,[1] and one moiety was vested in a family of the name of Dawnand. This was carried in marriage by Johanna daughter and heir of Peter Dawnand, to John Taverner.[2] In 1588, a fine was levied in which Richard Taverner, Gent., was querist, and William Taverner and Thomasine his wife, were deforciants, of a moiety of the manor of Dawnandussel with appurtenances, also 15 messuages, 15 tofts, 20 gardens, 15 orchards, 50 acres of land, 200 acres of meadow, 40 acres of pasture, 30 acres of wood, 200 acres of furze and heath, 200 acres of moor, and ten shillings rent with appurtenances in Carkeen, Dawnandussel, Dawnant Down,[3] Trevilye, Delmere, Trewsall, Medrees, St. Teath Church Town, St. Teath, Pengelly, Penpethy, Lanteglos, Trelights, St. Endellion, Trewynell, Treverledge, St. Adven, Bodmyn Borough, Camelford Borough, Greneborough, and Blysland; whereby, in consideration of the sum of £40 the aforesaid moiety was warranted to the said Richard Taverner.[4] It is manifest, however, that many of the lands here mentioned could not have been ancient tenements of the manor of Dawnant. In the same year Sir William Mohun died seized of forty acres of land in Largeyne and Dawnant.[5]

In 1566 John Tresunger suffered a fine in, inter alia, Dawnanbrode to John Roscarrock, whereby the said tenement was settled upon the said John Tresunger and his heirs to be held of the Chief Lord of the fee;[6] and in 1583 the said tenement, inter alia, was conveyed by the said John Tresunger to John Glanville,[7] who, in the following year, with Alice his wife suffered a fine in these lands, inter alia, to William Mathew,[8] and in 1590 the said lands were, inter alia, settled upon Richard Mathew.[9] In 1646 William Braddon, Esq., Richard Blight, and Loveday his wife and others suffered a fine in Dannonbrode and Trewynel to William Beale, Gent., when in respect to Dannonbrode the lands were warranted to the aforesaid William Beale by Richard Blight and Loveday his wife.[10]

The manor was clearly dismembered before the middle of the 17th century, but the tenement mentioned above as being in the possession of the Mohun family passed with the lands of that family to Mr. Pitt, who, as shewn by the terrier of 20th October 1727, claimed to make, by custom, in respect to these lands under the description of the Manor of Dennydizel, a payment of 5s. per annum in lieu of all manner of tithes,[11] and the several little tenements shewn in the Tithe Commutation Schedule as covered by this modus (ante p. 99) amount to 64 acres only. These lands are now the property of Hon. G. M. Fortescue of Boconnoc.

---

[1] See Hist. of Trigg under HAMATETHY, Vol. i, p. 354. [2] See Pedigree of Taverner, Post.

[3] In 1425, Dannonbrode, Dannondown, and South Pempethy, were held by John Cheynduit, as parcel of his Manor of Bodannan. Pedes Finium 3rd Henry VI, Easter.

[4] Pedes Finium, 30th Elizabeth, Trinity.   [5] Inquisition p.m., 30th Elizabeth, Easter.

[6] Pedes Finium, 30th Elizab., Easter.   [7] Ibid. 25th Elizab., Easter.

[8] Ibid 26th Elizab., Trinity.   [9] Ibid. 32nd Elizab., Trinity.

[10] Ibid. 22nd Charles, Michs.   [11] See ante p. 102.

MANOR OF ST. TEATH.

The manor of St. Teath, or St. Ethe, was held by Francis Buller, who by letters patent dated 1st March 1577-8[1] obtained a license to alienate, *inter alia*,[2] this manor to William Cornew, Gent., and Edward Symon, and accordingly in Easter term of the same year the said Francis Buller suffered a fine, *inter alia*, in this manor to the said William Cornew and Edward Symon and the heirs of the said William, and for this fine the said William and Edward afterwards remitted the said manor, &c., to the said Francis and his heirs to be held in capite by the services due and accustomed, but because this last remise was made without a license the lands became forfeited to the Crown. Upon payment however of a fine of 60s. the said Francis received a pardon, and the Queen granted the manor to him for herself, her heirs, and successors to be held in capite by the services due and accustomed.[3]

The manor, if it really ever possessed manorial privileges, is now dismembered.

TREWINNELL *alias* TREWINDLE *alias* TREWINNEW.

In the year 1646, a fine was levied in which William Beale, Gent., was querist, and William Braddon, Esq., Thomas Martin, Gent., Richard Blight, Esq., and Loveday his wife, William Hocken and Joyce his wife, and William Hocken son and heir apparent of the said William Hocken, were deforciants, by which, in consideration of a sum of £200, two messuages, &c., in Trewynell *alias* Trewyndle, Trewenta, and Dannanbrod, were conveyed to the said William Beale. It was probably a portion of the Carminow property.

[1] Rot. Pat., 20th Elizab., Part 3, m. 17.

[2] The other lands conveyed at the same time were the manors of Treglasta, Tregarreck, Kelliowe, and Pensight. These lands had formerly belonged to John Wydeslade of Tregarreck, who was attainted and executed at Tyburn for his connection with the rebellion of Humphry Arundell of Helland. Before his attainder, however, viz., in Easter term 36th Henry VIII, he suffered a recovery in these manors to John Cory and Richard Popham, who by their charter dated 31st May 36th Henry VIII (1544) demised the same to the said John Wydeslade and Agnes his wife for life, remainder to the heirs of the said John Wydeslade. The said John Wydeslade was seized also of the manor of Estcott and other lands, and by his charter dated 4th January 25th Henry VIII (1533-4) granted the same to a certain Robert Wydeslade and the heirs male of his body, in default remainder to the said John Wydeslade and his heirs. The reversion of these manors being therefore in the hands of the King by reason of the attainder of the said John Wydeslade by letters patent dated 14th Sept. 1552, the said reversion was granted to Reginald Mohun, Esquire for the Body, and his heirs and assigns for ever. (Rot. Pat., 6th Edw. VI, Part 9, m. 40.)

[3] Rot. Pat., 2nd Elizab., Part 5, m. 5.

William Beale eldest son of the abovementioned William, married Julianna daughter of Matthew Vivian of St. Adven, Gent., and resided at Trewinell, where he died in 1713, having by his will, dated 1st May 1712, devised Trewinell to his wife Julianna for life, with remainder, after her death, to his son Joseph Beale. It afterwards passed to Samuel Lyne of Launceston, together with Trehannick, and, like that estate, descended to George Fursdon of Fursdon, Esq., who by his will, dated 6th January 1771, and proved 14th January 1773, P.C.C., devised it, to trustees to the use of his wife Grace Fursdon for life, in lieu of dower, with remainder to his first and other sons, begotten of her, in tail male, with power of sale by the said trustees.

George Fursdon, by Grace his wife, had an only son named George Sydenham Fursdon, who died in 1837, leaving only one son surviving him, named George Fursdon, and no sale of this estate having been made by the trustees under the will of his grandfather, by his will, dated 22nd October 1872, he devised, *inter alia*, this estate to trustees to sell, who, by Indenture dated 25th March 1874, conveyed the same to Mr. William Teague of Trelisk near Truro, the present proprietor.

FAMILY HISTORY.

FAMILY OF DENNANT *alias* DAWNANT.

The manor of Dannant, or Dawnant, gave its name to a family which was long resident in the parish, and probably held this manor of the Chief Lords, though we are deficient of evidence upon the subject. Christopher Denaut was assessed to the subsidy in St. Teath in 1327.[1] In 1366 Warine Dannant was bailiff of the Hundred of Trigg.[2] In 1427 Roger Prideaux and Alice his wife suffered a fine in certain lands, in the parishes of St. Kew and St. Teath, to Otho Tregonan and Thomas Dawnant, by which the said lands were settled upon the said Roger and Alice for the term of their lives, with remainder to Otho Nicholls and Johanna his wife and the heirs of their bodies, in default remainder over to the right heirs of the said Alice.[3] In 1435 Thomas Dannand held lands in the manor of Treglasta of John Wydeslade and Elizabeth his wife. This Thomas would seem to have been related to the Bodulgate family, for in the charter of Walter Bodulgate of the last mentioned year for the endowment of the chapel of St. Thomas at Camelford we find him, in default of Thomas Roscarrock and Isabell his wife and Edward Coryton and Johanna his wife to fulfil the conditions of the charter, placed in remainder under the like limitations.[4] In 1442 he was one of the jurors on the Inquisition taken at Bodmin after the death of Sir William Bodrugan.[5] William Dawnand held lands in St. Teath of the value of 100s. per annum in 1521-3.[6] In 1544 Peter Tawnand (Dawnand) was assessed to the subsidy in St. Teath upon goods of the value of £5. Johanna his daughter and heir married John Taverner, to whom she would seem to have carried a moiety of the manor of Dawnandussel, for in 1588 a fine was levied of a moiety of that manor, in which Richard Taverner, Gent., was querist and William Taverner and Thomasine his wife were deforciants,[7] which

---

[1] Sub. Roll., 1st Edward III, $\frac{87}{7}$. See Appendix i.

[2] Ministers' Accounts. Duchy of Cornwall, 40th Edward III.

[3] Pedes Finium, 10th Henry VI, Michs.   [4] See Hist. of Trigg, Vol. ii, Appendix ii, p. 393.

[5] Inq. p.m., 20th Henry VI, No. 34.   [6] Return, Appendix ii.

[7] Pedes Finium, 30th Elizab., Trinity, see Pedigree of Taverner, post.

Richard and William are believed to have been her sons. The family of Taverner flourished at St. Teath for several descents, and became extinct on the death of Ann Taverner in 1774. John Downand, who was doubtless of the same family, held lands in Trevia, of the manor of Helston in Trigg in the parish of Lanteglos, which he surrendered to Johanna the wife of Christopher Walys, who in her right held them in 1604.[1]

LE BRUNE.

The family of Brune, or Le Brune, held, *inter alia*, the manor of Delioboll in this parish for a considerable period. In 1303, Robert le Brune, held one fee there of the fees of Moreton. This Robert married Isabella, relict of John de Lambrun. In 1302, John Coulyng and Margaret his wife, petitioned against Robert le Brune of Denlioubol, and Isabella his wife, concerning certain messuages in which they alleged the said Robert and Isabella had no ingress except by the demise of John Lambrun, formerly her husband.[2] At the same Assize the same John Coulyng sued them under the description of Robert le Delioubol and Isabella his wife, concerning one messuage and the moiety of one messuage in Trewoethen juxta Rosank and Treguson juxta Trewornenes, as the right of the said Margaret.[3] In 1337, Mathew the son of John Cok of Trelulla, Clerk, recovered from William the son of Robert Bruyn of Delyoubol, *inter alia*, one messuage, 60 acres of land, &c., in Trenewith juxta Tyntagel, and in 1346, William le Brune held in Delyoubol one fee of the fees of Moreton, which Robert his father had formerly held. This William, who attained equestrian rank, in 1387, settled his lands upon himself and the heirs of his body legitimately begotten, in default of such issue to the use of William Brune, Bastard, son of the said William Brune, Chr., and the heirs of his body legitimately begotten, and in default of such issue to the use of the right heirs of the said William Brune, Chr. The charters not having been duly executed, and the said William Brune, Chr., having died without legitimate issue, Alice Crewen, his sister, and Reginald Daling son of Johanna another sister, entered into possession of the estates. Alice Crewen had issue a son named Stephen, who left a daughter and heir called Johanna, who married Stephen Bodulgate.

In 1341, John Broun was one of the venditors of the ninth sheaf, &c., in the parish of St. Teath.[4]

[1] Assession Roll, Helston in Trigg, 44th Elizabeth.

[2] Assize Rolls, 30th Edward I, m. 34. At the same Assize we find the said John Coulyng and Margaret his wife, sueing: Thomas Petegru and Alice his wife, concerning the third part of two messuages in Wask juxta Maula and Talgoys juxta Trelegh; and William le Byry of Delyoubol and Johanna his wife, concerning the third part of two messuages in Relegh, the gift of John Lambrun her first husband, Ibid. 19.

[3] Ibid. m. 16.

[4] Inquisitiones Nonarum, p. 34. See ante p. 96.

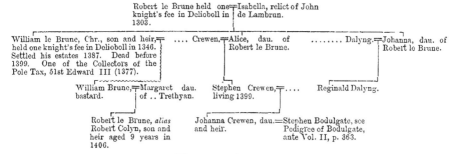

Robert le Brune held one⹂Isabella, relict of John
knight's fee in Delioboll in | de Lambrun.
1303.

William le Brune, Chr., son and heir,⹂ .... Crewen,⹂Alice, dau. of .... Dalyng.⹂Johanna, dau. of
held one knight's fee in Delioboll in 1346. | Robert le Brune. | Robert le Brune.
Settled his estates 1387. Dead before
1399. One of the Collectors of the
Pole Tax, 51st Edward III (1377).

William Brune,⹂Margaret dau. Stephen Crewen,⹂.... Reginald Dalyng.
bastard. | of .. Trethyan. living 1399.

Robert le Brune, alias Johanna Crewen, dau.=Stephen Bodulgate, see
Robert Colyn, son and and heir. Pedigree of Bodulgate,
heir aged 9 years in ante Vol. II, p. 363.
1406.

In January 1391-2, William Westcote and Johanna his wife, administrators of the goods of Stephen Brun, who died intestate, sued Dionisia who was the wife of John Ude of Pengelly (in St. Neot), and executrix of his will, in a plea of debt. (De Banco Roll, 15th Richard II, Hil., m. 180 d.)

TREHANNICK OF TREHANNICK.

The early history of this family is very obscure. As early as 1262 we find John de Trehonet and Katherine his wife joining with William de Dennant and Isabella his wife in the alienation of one messuage in Trehonet.[1] In 1302 a contention which had been before the courts of law was decided, wherein Johanna, who was the wife of Henry Stiner, recovered her dower of certain land in Setfenten against Agnes, who was the wife of John Cavel, which, Agnes stated, had been held by Henry Treonek her grandfather, whose heir she was.[2] In 1303 Mathew and Agnes Trehonet held in Trehonet half a knight's fee. In 1329 an assize of novel disseizin, in which Robert Trehonek was plaintiff and Roger Cavel and John Werying defendants, was postponed for default of jury. In 1337 Nicholas Trehanek[3] and Johanna Trehaverok held in Trehanek a small meadow and the bed of a mill there.[4] The relations which existed between the Trehannick and Trehaverock families, and their connection with Trehannick are very bewildering.[5] In 1321, an assize of view of recognizance was held to inquire if Johanna, who was the wife of John le Run, and Robert le Run had unjustly disseized John de Tynten, of his free tenements in Trehonek, Trevarthean, and Butcannek. Johanna answered as tenant, and said that a certain Mathew Treaverek, her brother, had died seized of the said tenements in his desmesne as of fee, after whose death she entered therein as his nearest heir without injury or disseizin to any one. John de Tynten said

[1] Pedes Finium, 46th Henry III, Michs. See also Hist. of Trigg, Vol. ii, p. 157.
    M)
[2] Assize Roll, 30th Edward I, 1 } 1. m. 20.
    21)
[3] Nicholas Treonak was one of the venditors of the ninth sheaf, &c. in the parish of St. Teath in 1341 See ante p. 96.   [4] Caption of Seizin, Black Prince.
[5] The Prebend of Trehaverock in the Church of St. Endellion, is called the Prebend of Trehaverock alias Trehannock, in the seventeenth century. See ante Vol. i, p. 506.

that the aforesaid Mathew by his charter granted all the said premises to the said John to hold for the term of his life, paying to the aforesaid Mathew and Johanna his wife, yearly, a rent of twelve marks during their lives with reversion, after the death of the said John de Tynten, of the said tenements to the aforesaid Johanna relict of John le Run, as sister and heir of the aforesaid Mathew; and, he said, that he was in full seizin, under the said charter, until the said Johanna and Robert unjustly disseized him, and he recovered his seizin with damages.[1] The knight's fee held by Mathew and Agnes Trehanek in 1303 had in 1346 passed to John Trehaverok.

We have not any further record of the family until 1469, when Nicholas Trehanek as kinsman and heir of Nicholas Trehanek and Johanna Trehaverok held the mill bed in Trehannek which the said Nicholas and Johanna had held in 1337, and Nicholas Trehanek held the same in 1491.[2] Nicholas had a son and heir named John, who, having taken part in the Cornish rising in favour of Perkin Warbec, was attainted by Act of Parliament on 25th January 1503. He does not appear to have accompanied the insurgents to Blackheath, but continued riotously assembled in arms. This attainder was, however, reversed by letters patent dated 16th Dec. 1607, in which he is described as John Treanek of Treanek in St. Etha, yeoman, called in the said Act John Trehannek. In 1521-3 he held lands in St. Teath of the value of 26s. 8d. per annum, and goods of the value of 100s. and arms for one man.[3] In 1539 he held the mill bed in Trehanek which Nicholas his father had held. He died before 1543, when Thomas his son was assessed to the subsidy in St. Teath upon goods of the value of £10. He died before 1553, in which year we find Johanna, Margery, and Dorothy Trehanek holding the mill bed in Trehanek which Thomas Trehanek, son and heir of John Trehanek, had taken at the previous assession. Johanna married John Bright, and at the assession of 1567, we find Ralph Mitchell holding two parts of the said mill bed by purchase from Margery and Dorothy two of the daughters and heirs of Thomas Trehanek, and the other part held by John Bright in right of Johanna his wife, the other daughter of the said Thomas. John Bright and his wife Johanna had issue an only daughter named Alice, who took to her husband Thomas Kelliowe, who, in 1574, in her right, held one portion of the aforesaid mill bed, whilst the other two portions continued to be held by Ralph Mitchell. Thomas Kellyowe was assessed to the subsidy in St. Teath in 1571 and 1594, and died 1st May 1596, leaving a son John Kylliowe, who, by surrender of Thomas his father, held a moiety of Trenhale, in the manor of Tyntagel, in 1617,[4] which, in 1627, was held by Eleanor his widow.

The name of Trehenneck still continued in St. Teath. Stephen Trehenneck had several children baptized there between 1559 and 1570, but, with one exception, a son named John, baptized in 1564, we trace them all to have been buried within the same period. Stephen himself, under the description of Stephen Trehinnick *alias* John Mill, was buried in 1593.[5]

[1] Assize Roll, 14th Edward II, 2 $\left.\begin{array}{l} N \\ 2 \\ 17 \end{array}\right\}$ 2. m. 12*d*.

[2] Assession Rolls, Manor of Helston in Trigg.   [3] See Appendix ii.

[4] Assession Rolls, Manor of Tyntagel.   [5] Parish Registers.

PEDIGREE OF TREHONET, *alias* TREHANEK, *alias* TREHANNICK OF TREHANNICK.

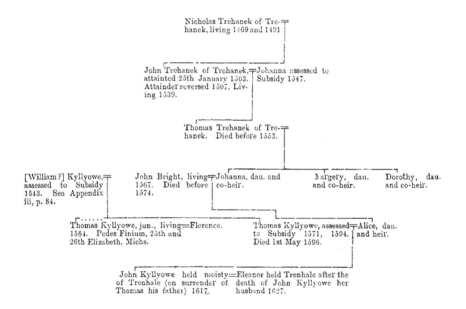

Nicholas Trehanek of Tre-⹀
hanek, living 1469 and 1491

John Trehanek of Trehanek,⹀Johanna assessed to
attainted 25th January 1503. Subsidy 1547.
Attainder reversed 1507. Liv-
ing 1539.

Thomas Trehanek of Tre-⹀
hanek. Died before 1553.

[William ?] Kyllyowe,⹀ John Bright, living⹀Johanna, dau. and   Margery, dau.   Dorothy, dau.
assessed to Subsidy   1567. Died before co-heir.   and co-heir.   and co-heir.
1543. See Appendix   1574.
iii, p. 84.

Thomas Kyllyowe, jun., living=Florence.   Thomas Kyllyowe, assessed⹀Alice, dau.
1584. Pedes Finium, 25th and   to Subsidy 1571, 1594. and heir.
26th Elizabeth, Michs.   Died 1st May 1596.

John Kyllyowe held moiety=Eleanor held Trenhale after the
of Trenhale (on surrender of death of John Kyllyowe her
Thomas his father) 1617.   husband 1627.

MEMORANDUM.—John Kelliowe and Jane Billing married at St. Tudy 1623.
  Richard son of John Kelliowe, bap. at St. Tudy 1624.
  Jane, dau. of John Killiow, Esq., late wife of Thomas Merrifield of St. Columb Major, died
    26th March. 1662, bur. at Michaelstow. (Hist. of Trigg, Vol. ii, p. 566).
  In 1412 William Kyllyowe held one ferling of land in Penhal and Trethack of William
    Botreaux, which land the said William Botreaux held of Stephen Trenouth in right of
    Margaret his wife (Inq. p.m., 13th Henry IV, No. 17).

U

PEDIGREE OF BEALE OF TREWINNEL.

William Beale of St. Maben=Elizabeth,dau. of John Tamlyn of St.
afterwards of St. Teath. | Maben, named in her father's will
| dated 16th Aug. 1670. Proved 3rd
| Nov. 1671. Mar. lic. 24th June 1658.
| Bur.[1] 6th Aug. 1682.

William Beale of Trewin-=Julianna, dau. of	Elizabeth,	John, bap[1].	John,	Mary,	Susanna,
nell in St. Teath, bap.[1] 8th	Mathew Vivian,	bap.[1] 6th	31st Dec-	bap.[1]	bap.[1]	bap.[1] 4th
Dec. 1668, bur.[1] 5th May	mar. at Advent,	Jan. 1673,	1675, bur.[1]	11th	20th	Aug. 1682,
1713. Will dated 1st May	21st April 1683.	bur.[1] 20th	13th Aug.	Mar.	June	bur.[1] 20th
1712, proved 22nd March	Bur.[1] 24th Dec.	Mar. 1690.	1678.	1671.	1676.	Sep. 1682.
1713-14. Archd. Cornw.	1727. See Hist.					
	of Trigg, Vol. ii, p.					
	162, 163					

Dorothy, bap.[1]	Mathew Beale of=Anne.	Joseph Beale, =Ann	Elizabeth, bap.[1]	William	John =Eliza-	Mary,
15th Jan.1683,	Trehannick, bap.[1]	bap.[1] 10th Mar.		2nd Oct. 1692,	Beale,	Beale.	beth.	bur.[2]
mar. at St.	30th Nov. 1687,	1689, bur.[1] 12th		bur.[1] 9th Feb.	son and	Bur.[2]		1746,
Maben Aug.	bur.[2] 15th Aug.	Nov. 1729. Will		1700.	heir.	3rd		unmar.
1716,to George	1727. Executor to	dated 5th Aug.			Bur.[1] 9th	July		
Fowler of Eg-	father's will. Will	1729. Prov. 27th		Juliana bap.[1]	Dec.	1738.		
loshayle.	dated 3rd Aug.	Feb. 1730.		29th May 1697,	1732, s.p.			
	1727. Prov.Archd.			bur.[1] 11th Oct.				
	Cornw.			1702.				

Mathew Beale	Anne Beale, a	Mathew,born	Grace, bap.[1]	Mary, born	John, bap.[2]	Elizabeth,
a minor on	minor on her	and bap.[1] 9th	8th Sept.1719	and bap. July	17th May	bap.[2] 2nd
his father's	father's death	Mar. 1717,		10th 1721,	1715.	April, 1718.
death.	bap.[1] 15th	bur.[1] 20th		bur.[1] 1746.		
	Oct. 1725.	April 1719.				

---

[1] At St. Teath.   [2] At Advent.

CARMINOW.

Considering the importance and dignity of this family its early history is very obscure, and from the lack of evidence in the public archives we are inclined to think that the family did not attain to any great celebrity until, at least, the end of the 13th century ; nevertheless as early as 1173 we find Roger de Carminow holding one knight's fee in Moteland, and nearly fifty years later : viz., about 1220, Roger de Carminow, perhaps son of the above, was witness to an undated charter relating to Trenant.[1] Early in the reign of King Henry III among those presented by the Sheriff of Cornwall as holding fifteen librates of land and more and not made knights is found the name of Robert de Carmeneu.[2] This Robert, who was possibly a son of the last named Roger, was witness to a charter in 1235,[3] and he was likewise, perhaps, the father of Roger Carminow, who married Sara daughter and coheir of Gervas de Hornicote. And because this marriage would seem to have added largely to the fortunes of the family it may be convenient, in this place, to give a brief account of the family of Hornicote.

Henry Fitz-Count, illegitimate son of Reginald de Dunstanville, Earl of Cornwall, received from King Henry II a grant of the whole County of Cornwall, to hold in farm, which grant was afterwards, in 1216, confirmed in fee. Henry Fitz-Count granted the manors of Hornicote and Tintagel to Gervas, called therefrom " de Hornicote," which Gervas, in 1198, was amerced, in Cornwall, for a breach of the Forest Laws.[4] In the following year he gave 100s. of fine to be excused from going beyond the seas with the king, and in addition, paid 41s. 8d. scutage for 2½ fees for the king's coronation.[5] In 1204 he paid scutage for five knights.[6] In the following year he paid a fine of twenty marks for the fees of five knights,[7] and in 1208, he gave two marks for a plea of forest.[8] In this year he died, for the sheriff accounted for forty marks received from Robert Tintaioel to have the whole of the inheritance which was Gervas de Hornicote's, his father.[9] In 1211, Robert Tintaiol accounted for the scutage of Scotland for four fees which had belonged to Roger de Mandeville ; and in the same year he paid eight marks of the scutage of Wales and had his discharge of 60s. of the Queen's gold. In 1214 Robert de Tintaioel paid scutage of 100s. for four fees.[10] In 1220 the Sheriff of Cornwall was commanded to resume into the King's hands all the lands which Henry Fitz-Count had given out of the King's demesnes to his knights and servitors during the time he held the County of Cornwall, *except the lands which belonged to Robert de Tintajel.*[11]

[1] Charter in the Muniment Room at Tregothnan.   [2] Cott. M.S. Claud. ii, fo. 30d.
[3] Charter at Tregothnan.   [4] Rot. Pip., 10th Richard I.
[5] Ibid. 1st John.   [6] Ibid. 5th John
[7] Ibid. 6th John   [8] Ibid. 9th John.   [9] Ibid. 9th John.
[10] Ibid. 16th John.   [11] Rot. Fin. 5th Henry III., m. 9.

U²

In 1223 Robert de Tintaiol paid 25s. for four fees of the scutage of Byham. He died before 31st March 1224, as appears from a writ directed to the Sheriff of Somerset, tested at Westminster on that day, in which W. Briwer, junr. is described as son and heir of Robert Tintajel;[1] though we find in the Cornish Roll for this year that the Sheriff accounted for five marks received from Robert Tintaioel for four fees of the scutage of Montgomery, and also for 25s. from Gervas de Tintaioel of the scutage of Byham, whilst the same Gervas had his discharge for the scutage of Bedford.[2] It would seem clear from this that Gervas was the successor of Robert in the Cornish fees, but we are unable to reconcile this record with that above cited, which describes W. Briwere as the son and heir of Robert Tintajel. Were there two persons of this name? However this may have been, in 1235, when the aid was granted to the King on the marriage of his sister Isabella to the Roman Emperor, Gervas de Tinthagel held in Hornicote with its appurtenances five fees,[3] and the collectors of the aid returned an account of £4 3s. 4d. from the five small fees of Gervase de Tintagel in Hornicote and Tintagel;[4] and at the same time Gervase de Tinthagel held in Merthin, Winianton, and in Thamarton, the 20th part of one small fee of the new feoffement of Richard Earl of Cornwall.[5] Gervas de Tintagel, or, as he was also called, Gervas de Hornicote left two daughters and coheirs named Cenota and Sara. The former married and had issue, a daughter named Margery, who died s.p., when her Aunt Sara became her heir. Sara married Roger Carminow[6] as above stated, and left four children, John, Roger, Gervas, and Maud, or Lucy, who married Robert de Helligan, John dying s.p. Roger became heir to both his father and mother,[7] and in 1300 held one fee in Hornicote of the annual value of £25, and the 20th part of one fee in Tamerton, Wynyenton, and Merthyn held of Edmund Earl of Cornwall.[8]

---

[1] Rot. Claus. 8th Henry III. It would seem probable that Gervas de Hornicote was a Cadet of the Baronial family of Briwere. William de Briwere was Sheriff of Devon for ten years in succession, 1179—1189, of Cornwall 1202 and 1203; and of Dorset and Somerset 1209 and 1210. He was a nobleman of great power and influence with King John, and had possessions in Cornwall. His son died s.p.m., leaving five co-heirs, one of whom, Alice, married Reginald de Mohun. The elder William was cousin of William Briwere, Bishop of Exeter. In an ancient undated charter, John, son of Anthony de la Briwere, grants to Ranulphus Giffard lands in Donethly; Roger Carmenow, Richard Peverel, Odo St. Winnow, and others being witnesses. (Penes Sir W. C. Trevelyan, Bart.)

[2] Rot. Pip. 8th Henry III.   [3] Testa de Nevil, p. 187.   [4] Ibid. p. 201.

[5] Ibid. fo. 187. In 1208, Meredin and Winienton were held by Cadwalanus Wallensis, who died in 1211, when his lands were taken into the King's hands. They were afterwards granted by King Henry III. to his brother Richard Earl of Cornwall, who being desirous of recovering Tintagel, which, as we have seen above, had been alienated from the Earldom, gave them, together with the Manor of Tamarton, to Gervas de Hornicote in exchange for the Manor of Bochyny (Tintagel). (Assize Roll, 30th Edward I. 1 M/21 {2. m. 22.)

[6] In 1235, Roger Carminow held 1 acre of land in Dobelboys, containing one carucate Cornish. (Testa de Nevil, p. 201.)

[7] Assize Roll Cornwall, 30th Edw. I. 1 M/21 {1. m. 16. Benedikt Tintagel is mentioned in 1285 (Fin. Roll 13th Edw. I.)

[8] Inq. p.m. Edmund, Earl of Cornwall, 28th Edw. I. No. 44.

Roger de Carminow, last mentioned, in 1283 was plaintiff in a suit against Peter de Lancuk concerning certain lands in East and West Dysart, in which he alleged the said Peter had no ingress except by William Lancuk, who thereof unjustly disseized Sara Hornycote, mother of the said Roger, whose heir he is, and he recovered seizin.[1] He became a person of considerable importance. In 1284 he was amerced for that he held one entire knight's fee, was of full age, and had not been made a knight.[2] In 1296 Sir Roger de Carminou was summoned to perform military service in person against the Scots.[3] In 1297 he was returned by the Sheriff of Cornwall as holding lands or rents of the annual value of £20 and upwards, and as such summoned under the general writ to perform military service with horses and arms, &c., in parts beyond the seas.[4] In 1296 he paid the scutage for Wales.[5] In 1300 he was knight for the shire in Parliament, and had his writ "de expensis."[6] In 1301 Sir Roger de Carmynow was witness to a charter of Thomas de Pridias, Lord of Penstradou, granting to Odo de Rupe three Cornish acres of land in the ville of Skeysmore, and in the following year he was witness to two charters relating, respectively, to Killiganoun and Trevilla.[7] In 1301 he was summoned from Cornwall to perform military service in person against the Scots,[8] and in the following year he was again knight for the shire in Parliament,[9] and had his writ "de expensis" on 20th October.[10] In 29th Edward I (1301) Roger de Carminow held in Trelowith and Eglosros one fee value £8.[11] He died in 1308 seized of the manors of Wynyenton and Merthen, which same manors, together with the manor of Tamerton which Martin de Fishaer held for the term of his life, were held by the said Roger in capite of the Earldom of Cornwall by the service of the twentieth part of one knight's fee, and Oliver Carminow his son was found to be his nearest heir and to be of the age of 30 years and more.[12] He had also several other sons and a daughter named Johanna, who married William de Whalesburgh,[13] as appears from a fine levied in 1319, in which Oliver de Caermenou and Elizabeth his wife were querists, and Mathew de

[1] Assize Roll, 11th Edward I. $1\frac{M}{20}$ } 3. m. 14.

[2] Assize Roll, Cornwall, $1\frac{M}{20}$ } 5. m. 11.

[3] Rot. Claus., 28th Edward I, m. 12d.

[4] Cott. M.S., Claud ii, fo. 64.

[5] Rot. Pip., 25th Edward I.

[6] Rot. Claus., 28th Edward I, m. 12d.

[7] Charters at Tregothnan.

[8] Rot. Claus., 29th Edward I, m. 12d & 13.

[9] Parl. Writs.

[10] Rot. Claus., 30th Edward I, m. 3d.

[11] Extent of the Fees of Joceus de Dinham, Inq. p.m. 29th Edward I, No. 56.

[12] Inq. p.m., 2nd Edward II, No. 73.

[13] Several settlements would seem to have been made upon this marriage. By his charter dated in the feast of St. Gregory the Pope 5th Edward II, William de Whalesbrew granted to John de Carmynow the manor of Udnow and the advowson of the Church of St. Piran for the life of the said William; and by a charter dated on Wednesday in the feast of St. Valentine 6th Edward II, John Carmynow, knight, regranted to William de Whalesbury and Johanna his wife the same premises, to hold to the said William and Johanna, their heirs and assigns for ever; and by a further charter, dated at Bodconek, on Wednesday next before the feast of SS. Tiburcius and Valerianus 6th Edward II, John Carminow, Knt., granted to the said William de Whalesbreu and Johanna his wife, and to the heirs and assigns of the said William, all the lands of the said John in Whalesbreu, all his lands in Treros, together with the advowson of the Church of St. Maunan and divers other Whalesbrew lands. This charter is sealed with the arms of Carminow: Az. a bend or, in chief a label of five points, with the legend, "S. IOH'IS CARMINO." (Charters at Nettlecomb Park, Co. Somerset.)

Penfern, clerk, deforc. by which the Manor of Carmenou and certain other Manors and Advowsons were settled upon the said Oliver and Elizabeth and the heirs of their bodies, in default remainder to John brother of the said Oliver and the heirs of his body, in default remainder to Richard brother of the said John and the heirs of his body; in default remainder to Minanus brother of Richard and the heirs of his body, in default remainder to William de Whalebreus and Johanna his wife and the heirs of the bodies of the said William and Johanna, and in default of such issue, remainder to the right heirs of the said Oliver.[1]

Sir Oliver de Carmenou was Knight of the Shire for Cornwall in 1313, and had his writ "de expensis;"[2] and in 1324 he was returned by the Sheriff of Cornwall, as possessed of lands to the amount of £40 per annum and upwards, and so was summoned by general proclamation to attend the great Council at Westminster in May of that year,[3] and in 1326 he was appointed one of the Commissioners of Array for Cornwall in the place of one not able to act.[4]

In 1332 Oliver Carminow is stated to owe 60s. 9d. of aid beyond 25s. which he had paid for each of four fees, and four parts of a fee.[5]

By charter dated Wednesday next before the feast of St. Ambrose (1st April) 11th Edward III (1337), Oliver Carmynow, Knt. granted the Manors of Wynyanton and Kenel to Roger Carmynow, his son, at the annual rent of £1 6s. 8d. during the life of the said Oliver, and after his decease to hold the said manors to the said Roger and the heirs of his body; in default remainder to Thomas his brother and the heirs of his body; in default remainder to John, brother of Thomas, and the heirs of his body; in default remainder to Richard, brother of the said John, and the heirs of his body; in default remainder to the right heirs of Roger.[6]

The marriages of this Oliver are very confused and uncertain. He would seem to have had three wives, and it is difficult to define, with exactness, except as regards the first, the issue derived from each wife. In the Inquisition taken on Tuesday next before the feast of St. George the Martyr 20th Henry VI, in which is recited the fine of 12th Edw. II, abstracted above, and a fine, levied in Easter term following, between the same parties, in which the same lands were further settled upon Johanna, relict of John Arundell (mother of Oliver) to hold in dower, remainder after the death of the said Johanna to the said Oliver and Elizabeth, and the *heirs of their bodies*, which Oliver and Elizabeth, it is continued, had issue, Roger, Elizabeth, and Matilda, and then is recited the marriage of, and descent from, each, as shewn in the annexed pedigree.[7] This Elizabeth, wife of Oliver, was Elizabeth Pomeroy,

---

[1] Pedes Finium 12th Edward II. Trinity.   [2] Rot. Claus. 7th Edw. II m. 20 d.

[3] Cott. MS. C. ii fo. 45.   [4] Rot. Pat. 19th Edward II Part 1, m 1.

[5] Rot. Pip. 7th, Edw. III.

[6] The seal to this charter is without the label, and bears the legend in Gothic letters "SIGILVM OLIVERI CARMINO." Another charter, dated in 16th Edward III, by which Oliver Carminow and Roger his son confirm the above grant, bears the seals of both Oliver and Roger, the former without any label, and the latter having one of five points.

[7] Inq., p.m. 20th Henry VI, No. 36.

and it might be inferred that he had no other issue by her than is named above, nevertheless it would, from various circumstances, seem probable that Oliver's other sons Thomas, John, and Richard were by his first wife. Thomas, who in 1351 is described as " Magister," as having a standing in the Schools,[1] was instituted to the Rectory of Maugan, on 6th August 1349, upon the presentation of John de Whalesborow, and on 7th December 1361 was succeeded there by Richard Karyorghel, but whether the benefice became void by the death or resignation of the said Thomas is not stated in the registers.[2] John and Richard, as shewn by the settlement above cited, were living in 1337, but died s.p. By his second marriage with Isolda, daughter of Reginald Ferrers,[3] son of William Ferrers by Isolda de Cardinan, relict of Thomas de Tracy, Oliver Carminow had two other daughters named Margery and Johanna. Margery was taken to wife by Simon Berkele, and Johanna married John Petit, the descents from whom are proved by the Inquisition taken after the death of John Cheynduit in 1426.[4] Oliver also, we think, probably late in life, married a third wife, but of her we have no knowledge.[5]

Oliver was succeeded by his son, Sir Roger Carminow, who, by charter dated Wednesday next before the feast of St. John Baptist (18th June) 22nd Edward III (1348), granted to Thomas de Faune and John Kendell the aforesaid manors, reserving the wood of Kenel.[6] Roger's issue failed on the death of his great grandaughter, Johanna Carminow, in 1395-6, when John Arundell of Lanherne, the grandson of Sir Roger's sister Elizabeth, and John Trevarthian, the son of his sister Matilda, were found to be his nearest heirs.

We shall now return to Sir John Carminow, the younger son of Roger son of Sara Hornicote. He married Johanna, daughter and heir of Sir John Glyn and acquired her estates. In 1320 he made fine for the confirmation of certain deeds.[7] In 1324 we find him advanced to the degree of a Knight and returned by the Sheriff of Cornwall as holding lands, &c., to the amount of £40 a year or upwards, and he was accordingly summoned by general proclamation to attend the Great Council at Westminster.[8] On 10th October 1331 he was granted the custody of the royal forests, parks, woods, and warrens, in Cornwall, but he died very soon afterwards for his writ " diem clausit extremum " was issued on the following month.[9] And on 20th January 1333-4, the Bishop of Exeter issued

[1] Assize Roll, 25th Edward III, $\frac{N}{2}$ $\left.\begin{array}{c} \\ \\ 23\end{array}\right\}$ 6 m. 56 d.

[2] Bishops' Registers, Exeter.

[3] In 6th Henry VI, Thomas Carminow held one-fourth of a fee in West Dissart which John de Ferrers once held.

[4] Inq. p.m., 6th Henry VI, No. 57. See Hist. of Trigg, Vol. I, pp. 544, 546.

[5] Since the statement in the text has been in type, the author's conjecture has been confirmed by his discovery of a note from the Diocesan Registers, which shews that, on 21st April 1335, proceedings were taken against William Trenewith, Priest, relative to a clandestine marriage between Sir Oliver Carminow, Knt., and a certain Sibell celebrated by the said William in the Chapel of Carminow, which resulted in the said William being absolved. (Bishop Grandisson's Register Vol. ii, fo. 190).

[6] Charters penes J. J. Rogers, of Penrose, Esq., now Lord of the Manor of Wynyanton.

[7] Rot. Fin., 14th Edward H, m.

[8] MS. Cott. Claud. C. ii, fo. 45.

[9] Rot. Fin. 5th Edward III.

a mandate to revoke the acceptance, by the Archdeacon of Cornwall, of the will of John de Carmynow, Knt.[1]   He had, by his wife Johanna,[2] four sons, Roger, Thomas, Reginald, and Walter, and a daughter Margaret, who married John Beaupre.   Roger, Thomas and Reginald died s.p. and v.p., and Walter succeeded his father.

In 1337 Johanna, who was the wife of John Carmynew, Kut., and Walter, son of the same Johanna, and John Dyngelly were sued by Nicholas, son of John de Bethbole, for unjustly disseizin him of a free tenement in Bethbole juxta Tretheven[3] (in St. Kew, see Hist. of Trigg, vol. ii, p. 141), but Nicholas did not recover.[4]

Sir Walter Carminow, son and heir of Sir John, married Alice, daughter of Sir Stephen de Tinten by Elizabeth one of the two daughters of Alan Bloyou, and sister and coheir of Ralph Bloyou, who died s.p.   Sir Stephen de Tinten left a son and heir named Ralph, whose wardship and marriage were in 1321 granted by the Bishop of Exeter to Ralph Bloyou, and if the said Ralph, son of Stephen, did not live to marry, the Bishop granted to the said Ralph Bloyou the marriage of Alice and Johanna sisters and heirs of the said Ralph de Tinten.[5]   He died s.p., and his sisters inherited his lands.

We have made frequent mention of the name of Bloyou, and inasmuch as this family, for many descents, was of considerable importance in Cornwall, and particularly connected with the Deanery of Trigg, we propose here to give a short account of it.

The family of Bloyou was descended from Blohinus, who held several manors in Cornwall at the time of the Domesday Survey.   The name has been variously written. Richard Bloio was a witness to a charter between 1193 and 1202,[6] and was probably the same Richard who was amerced in 1203.[7] Gervas Bloyou gave 100 marks for a plea of forest in 1207.[8]   These were probably younger brothers of Alan Bloyou, who held seven fees in Cornwall for which he paid scutage in 1186,[9] and who is named in 1196.[10]   This Alan died in 1204, in which year Henry Bloyou paid his relief for the seven fees which his father Alan had held in Cornwall.[11]   Henry died s.p., and was succeeded by his brother Ralph, who in 1210 gave sixty marks and a palfrey to have the seven fees which Henry his brother had held, and for these seven fees Ralph paid scutage in 1222 and 1225.   Ralph was succeeded by another Alan, who by [Johanna ?] the eldest daughter of Sir Henry Bodrugan had a son Ralph, whose son Alan married Johanna daughter and heir of Sir Peter Nauskoyk, or Nanskew.   After

---

[1] Bishop Grandisson's Register, Vol. ii, fo. 177.

[2] On 19th April 1332. The Lady Johanna, relict of Sir John Carmynow, Knt., had licence to celebrate Divine Service in the Oratory in her manor of Glyn. (Bishop Grandisson's Reg., Vol. ii, fo. 150.)

[3] Assize Roll, 11th Edward III $\frac{N}{2}$ 4 m. 111.

[4] In 1327 John Carmynou was assessed to the subsidy in the parish of St. Kew at the highest rate in the parish. Sub. Roll, 1st Edward III $\frac{7}{87}$ See Appendix iii, Hist. of Trigg, Vol. ii, p. 276.

[5] Bishop Grandisson's Reg., Vol. ii, fo. 27 d.

[6] Tregothnan Charters.   [7] Rot. Fin. 5th John.

[8] Ibid. 9th John.   [9] Red Book of the Excheq., fo. 59d.

[10] Rot. Pip., 8th Richard I.   [11] Rot. Fin., 6th John.

the death of Alan Bloyou she married Walter Bluet, and by a fine levied in 1324, thirty-four messuages, including, *inter alia*, Nanskoyk Magna and Nanskoyk Parva, were settled upon the said Walter and Johanna during the life of Johanna and after her death upon the aforesaid Ralph Bloyou and the heirs of his body, and in default of such issue, remainder to the right heirs of the said Johanna.[1] Alan Bloighou, who died 1305, left by the said Johanna a son named Ralph, who was born on the 23rd July 1297, and two daughters, Elizabeth and Johanna. In 1331 Ralph Bloyou had attained equestrian rank, for in that year we find that the Bishop of Exeter granted to Sir Ralph Bloyou, Kut., a license to celebrate the Divine Offices in his Chapel of St. Elette, within the parish of St. Endellion, by Sir Richard de Pont, priest, with the expressed consent of Mr. Richard de Carburra, of the said Church Rector of a Portion.[2] Ralph died s.p., and his sisters became his heirs.[3] Elizabeth married first Sir Stephen de Tinten, by whom she had a daughter Alice, who became the wife of Sir Walter Carminow ; and secondly she took to her husband Ralph Beaupel, *alias* Beaupre, *alias* Bello Prato. In 1355 John Shyrlek, the Guardian of the Fees of the Duchy of Cornwall, accounted for £6 13s. 4d. of relief of Ralph Beaupel and Elizabeth his wife for two fees of Moreton in Tregowell, which fees are stated to be members of the six fees of Polrode.[4] On 1st October 1359, it was ordered by the Council of the Duke of Cornwall that all charters and muniments belonging to the late Ralph Bloyou should be delivered to Ralph Beaupel, whose possessions had come to him in right of Elizabeth his wife.[5] Ralph Beaupre had, perhaps by another wife, a daughter who married Sir Thomas Carminow. We do not know to whom Johanna, the younger sister of Ralph Bloyou was married, but she had a daughter named Margery who was the mother of Simon Berkle who espoused Margery daughter of Sir Oliver Carminow. According to the inquisition post mortem of John Cheynduit of Bodannan, taken 28th May 1427, Simon Berkle had a son Bartholomew, who had a son Benedict, who was the father of Johanna the mother of the said John Cheynduit. But in a suit in Banco in 1411, between Margaret, relict of Sir William Carminow, and John Cheynduit, concerning certain lands which the said Margaret claimed to hold in dower, it is pleaded by John Cheynduit, as regards one carucate of land in Bodowe, that a certain Richard le Fleming gave the said land to one Benedict Berkle and the heirs of his body, and that the same land,

---

[1] Pedes Pinlum, 18th Edward II, Michs.

[2] Bishop Grandisson's Reg., Vol. ii, fo. 32. This is our first knowledge of Mr. Richard de Carburra being a Portioner of St. Endellion. He probably succeeded Mr. Richard de St. Margaret, who was a Portioner in 1312. (See Hist. of Trigg, Vol. i, p. 490). The Carburras succeeded the St. Margarets in their estates. (Ibid, p. 274).

[3] Inq. p.m., 34th Edward I, No. 44, and 9th Edward II, No. 69. The following Clerks of the name of Bloyou, whose places we cannot fix in the pedigree, we find mentioned in the Episcopal Registers. On 29th February 1308 Benedict Bloyou was instituted to the Church of St. Tudy. Bp. Stapeldon's Reg., fo. 28.

1309, Roger de Bloyou Rector of Monk's Okehampton.

1317, 5th Kal. May—Mr. John Bloyou was collated to a Prebend in Exeter Cathedral. Bp. Stapeldon's Reg., fo. 118.

1320, Licence of absence was granted to Mr. John Bloyou, Rector of St. Columb Major.

[4] Ministers' Accounts Duchy of Cornwall, 29th Edward III.

[5] Council Book of the Black Prince, 33rd Edward III. Elizabeth Beaupre survived her second husband. On 9th October 1371 the Bishop granted to her his licence to have Divine Services celebrated in her presence in the Chapels wheresoever in her manors.

v

after the death of the said Benedict, and Bartholomew, son and heir of the same Benedict, and Margaret, sister of the said Bartholomew, to the said John, son of the said Margaret, and kinsman and heir of the aforesaid Bartholomew, ought to descend.[1] This descent of Berkle differs from that heretofore given in the transposition of Benedict and Bartholomew as father and son, and it might be presumed that as this last mentioned record is earlier, and relates to a plea of lands, it would be more likely to be correct than the inquisition taken 16 years afterwards. Nevertheless such was not the case, as appears from the devolution of Cant in St. Minver.[2]

Sir Walter Carminow by his wife Alice de Tinten had two sons, Ralph and William. Ralph married first Katherine, daughter and coheir of Sir William Champernon, and relict of [Sir Walter?] Wodeland. They were in some way related, for on 14th June 1372 the Bishop granted a licence for the marriage, the parties being within the prohibited degrees.[3] Elizabeth, the sister of Katherine, became the wife of John Sergeaux. The following proceedings form an apt illustration of the turbulent character of the period : In 1377 Ralph Carminow, Knight, and William his brother petitioned the King in Council complaining that William Champernon was seized of certain manors, &c., and had two daughters, and died; after whose death the said two daughters entered into possession of the said manors, &c., and made partition between them, one daughter was married to the said Ralph, and the other to John Sergeaux, which John, covetous to have the whole inheritance, sent divers persons to the manors of the said Ralph at Bockonnoc, and there beat and illtreated him and his wife, and carried away their goods to the value of £200, leaving the said Ralph for dead. Then Ralph gave this manor, which had been allotted to his wife, to divers persons for the term of his life at a certain rent, who let their estate to the said William Carminow, who let the same to Ralph for a term of years yet unexpired, whereupon the said John Sergeaux, being Sheriff of Cornwall, with a great number of persons armed, under the colour of his office, entered into the manors of the said William, which he had of the portion of Ralph's wife, and the other lands, &c., of Ralph, and took goods and chattels of the value of £1000, and they pray for a remedy.[4]

Katherine, wife of Sir Ralph Carminow, died without issue, and upon this ground, and because the said Ralph died without leaving heirs of his body, in January 1393–4, Elizabeth her sister and heir, relict of John Sergeaux, sought to recover certain lands in Jacobstow which had been settled upon the said Ralph and Katherine and the heirs of their bodies and the heirs of the body of the said Ralph.[5] By his second marriage, however, Ralph had a daughter Alice who is named in his will, without date,[6] but she predeceased him, for on his death, on 9th October 1386, his brother William was found to be his nearest heir.

[1] De Banco Roll, 12th Henry IV, Trinity m. 386.   [2] See Hist. of Trigg, Vol. iii, p. 56.
[3] Bishop Brantingham's Reg., fo. 22.
[4] Petitions to the King in Council, c. 1562, 1563, writ dated 10th December 1st Richard II.
[5] De Banco Roll, 17th Richard H, Hil. m. 244 d.
[6] Proved at Lambeth, 31st January 1386-7.   [7] Inq. p.m. 10th Richard II, No. 11.

Sir William Carminow[1] left four sons, John, Thomas, Nicholas, and Walter. John left one son of the same name, who died 6th May 1420, s.p., when his uncle Thomas was found to be his nearest heir.[2] Thomas, by his wife Johanna relict of Otho Trevarthian, left two daughters who at the time of their father's death were both married : Margaret, the elder, to Hugh Courteney, to whom, *inter alia*, she carried Boconnoc, and Jane the younger to Thomas Baron Carew,[3] after whose death she remarried Halnathan Mauleverer. Nicholas Carminow, the third son of Sir William, died in 1471 s.p.,[4] when Johanna wife of Halnathan Mauleverer was found to be his nearest heir ;[5] Consequently the representation of the family of Carminow devolved upon the younger son Walter, who married Jane daughter and heir of Richard Resprin of Resprin, in St. Winnow. He would seem to have dwelt in St. Pinnock, for on 13th June 1437 a licence was granted to Walter Carminow, Esq., and Johanna his wife to celebrate Divine Service in the Church of All Saints in that parish on the feasts of All Saints and St. Kaine, and also on the three Rogation Days and the 10th May.[6] They had two sons. John his eldest son married another heiress : viz., Phillippa daughter and coheir of John Trenewith of Fentengollen, where the family afterwards seated themselves for two or three descents. He died in 1492, and by his will directed that his body should be buried in the Priory Church of St. Mary and St. Petroc of Bodmin, and he gave legacies to the vicar of St. Winnow for tithes forgotten, to the poor Hospital of St. Lawrence at Launceston, to the poor Hospital of St. Anthony, and the poor Chapel of St. George at Bodmin. He had a large family, but two of his sons, only, left issue. John his son and heir died in 1547 s p., and directed that his body should be buried in the Church of St. Michael Penkevil. He left legacies to the Hospitals of St. Lawrence, St. Anthony, and St. George at Bodmin, and bequeathed all his lands not already settled to his nephew John Carmynow son of Thomas Carminow his brother as his next of kin. Thomas Carminow was Gentleman Usher of the Chamber to King Henry VIII, and he had several grants from the Crown. On 11th September 1509 he was appointed Constable of the Castle and Keeper of the Park at Restormel,[7] and on 13th February following he was granted the manor of Bliston in farm.[8] In 1528 he took two tenures within the Park of Restormel formerly in the tenure of John Swete, because John Cryppis, late tenant there, had forfeited the same for destroying the game.[9] He died in 1528 and by his will directed that his body should be buried in the Church of the Grey Friars at Bodmin, "before the Aulter of John Carminow," and he gave to the Grey Friars "for the place where I shall be buried 10s." By a codicil dated 12th June 1528 he directs that his wife Elizabeth shall have all the lands which he had recently purchased in

---

[1] On 28th May 1397 Sir William Carmynow and Margaret his wife had licence for an Oratory at Bokonek. (Bishop Stafford's Reg., fo. 12).

[2] Inq. p.m., 8th Henry V, No. 99.   [3] Inq. p.m., 21st Henry VI, No. 46.

[4] On 21st September 1432 Nicholas Carmynow and Alice his wife had licence to celebrate Divine Service within their mansion of Huston. (Bishop Lacy's Reg.)

[5] Inq. p.m., 11th Edward IV., No. 44.   [6] Bishop Lacey's Register, Vol. iii, fo. 144.

[7] Rot. Pat., 1st Henry VIII, Part 1, m. 20.   [8] Ibid. Part 2, m. 34. See Hist. of Trigg, Vol. i, p. 32.

[9] Assession Roll, Restormel, 20th Henry VIII.

V²

Temple and St. Breward of John Netherton. His widow Elizabeth married Edward Clyker, for in 1545 Edward Clyker held the two tenements above mentioned in Restormel Park in right of Elizabeth relict of Thomas Carmynow.[1]

Nicholas Carminow, youngest son of the abovementioned John, upon whom his mother settled Trenewith, left two daughters, Elizabeth, the elder, married Nicholas Herle of Trenouth, and Phillippa, the younger, married 1st Hugh Boscawen of Tregothnan and afterwards James Trewinard.

Whilst John Carminow, eldest son and heir of Thomas Carminow, elder brother of the last named Nicholas, inherited Fentengollen, Nicholas the second son had Resprin. He died in 1569, leaving a daughter and heir, named Grace, who became the wife of Richard Prideaux of Theuborough, who, in her right, enjoyed Resprin. Nordon describes Polmawgan as " the howse of Thomas Carmyno," and " Repryn," as " the howse of Richard Prydiaux."[2] In 1609 Jonathan Prideaux, son and heir of Richard and his wife Grace, and Winifred his wife, William Salter, Esq. and Ann his wife and Philip Cole and Margaret his wife suffered a fine by which the manor of Carburra and Respryn were released to Thomas Carmynow, their kinsman,[3] who in 1611, again alienated Resprin.

John Carminow, the last abovementioned, died in 1592. In his will, which was dated at Husten on 27th January 30th Elizabeth (1588) he described himself as of Fentengollen. He makes his wife Margaret and his son Oliver joint executors, and gives to his wife certain estates for life, remainder to his youngest son Juell and the heirs of his body, in default of such issue remainder to Thomas Carminow and the heirs of his body, in default remainder over to his own right heirs. He gives also to his son Juell his manors of Cant and Tremore with like limitations—names his daughter Mary Flamank and her husband William and gives to their children, Oliver, Charles, and Katherine, lands or legacies—to Charles he bequeaths one tenement in Temple held by George Sturtridge. To his son Oliver he gives the manor of Pendogatt, and he binds his sons severally, under pain of forfeiture, not to alienate. He omits to mention his second son George Carminow,[4] though he devises lands to Thomas, who was the eldest son of the said George.

Oliver Carminow, by deed dated 10th May, 25th Elizabeth (1593), released to Frances Carnsew of Bokelly an annual rent of 12s. reserved by John Carminow on a grant of lands in Bokelly to one William Carnsew, by deed dated 6th November 13th Edward IV.[5] He left no male issue, and the representation of the family devolved upon Thomas Carminow the son of George by Jane daughter of John Lower of Polmaugan in St. Winnow. Thomas Carminow sold Resprin in 1611, and settled at Trehannick in St. Teath,[6]

[1] Assession Roll, Restormel, 37th Henry VIII.

[2] Nordon, p. 88.   [3] Ped. Fin. 7th James, Easter.

[4] A George Carminow was Steward of the Duchy manor of Penlyne in 39th Elizabeth. (Ministers' Accounts.)

[5] The seal of arms to this deed is without the label, and is surmounted by the crest, the whole surrounded by the legend " CALA RAGGI WHETHLOW."

[6] Subsidy Roll, 4th Charles.

where he was assessed to the subsidy in 1628, and was buried in 1640, having in 1630 expended a considerable sum in reparing the Church and erecting a tower thereto.[1] Administration of his goods was granted on 20th October in that year to William Carminow his second son, but the amount of the inventory of his personal effects was £35 17s. 8d. only. Thomas the eldest son would appear to have died in the Upper Bench Prison in London, in 1651, on the 1st June in which year administration of his effects was granted to William Hunt, as principal creditor. The amount of the debt was £1000, Hunt being at that time Commander of a ship of war in Scotland. The grant of adminstration was opposed by a certain Gilbert Clerke. The will of a certain Catherine Carmynow, of the Parish of St. Paul's, Covent Garden, widow, dated 11th February 1695, was proved 15th December 1696. She gave all her personal estate whatsoever to her trusty friend Benjamin Jeffreys, Esq., to be disposed of at his discretion, and appointed him sole executor. This Catherine was, probably, the widow of the last mentioned Thomas. William son of Thomas succeeded him in Trehannick, and left a son of his own name, born in 1643. In 1667 he joined in the sale of Trehannick, subsequent to which date we lose sight of him. And this ancient family in him is believed to have become extinct.

ARMS: The arms usually assigned to the family of Carminow are: *az., a bend or, in chief a label of three points gu.* And it has been generally received that the label was added in consequence of the Scrope and Grosvenor controversy. It was found that three families claimed the same arms: Scrope, Grosvenor, and Carminow, and in 1389 a Court of Chivalry was held to determine the right of the several claimants, the trial in respect to which lasted four years. In the case of Scrope *versus* Grosvenor, the latter was forbidden to carry the arms unless he differenced them with a bordour or, which he refused to do, and assumed, instead, a new coat: *az. a garb or*, but the contest between Scrope and Carminow was not conclusive, and ultimately both families were allowed to bear the same arms. There are a number of ancient Carminow seals extant without the label, and we find that the latter was used before the controversy with Scrope arose. As an illustration: to a Charter of 16th Edward III, the seals of Oliver Carminow and his son Roger are still appendant, the seal of the father being without the label, whilst that of the son is charged with one of five points. To a deed as late as 25th Elizabeth (1593) Oliver Carminow of Fentengollen uses a seal without a label, and circumscribed with the legend "CALA RAGGI WHETHLOW."

---

[1] See ante, pp. 20, 21.

Note.—The pedigree of the family of Carminow recorded in the Heralds' College is very inaccurate, but a revised pedigree has recently been printed by the Harleian Society in the Visitation of Cornwall, edited by Lieut. Colonel Vivian and Dr. Drake. It is to that astute and learned genealogist, the latter of those gentlemen, that we are specially indebted for that valuable addition to Cornish genealogy; the pedigree being based upon authentic evidence, collected by great labour, is, as far as it goes, in most respects very accurate.

PEDIGREE OF THE FAMILIES OF

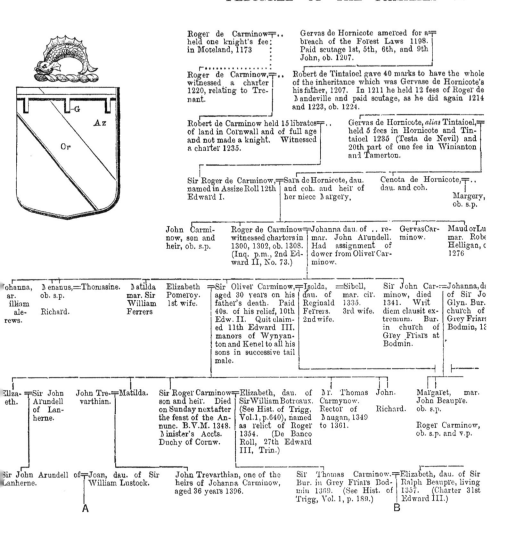

Roger de Carminow ⊤.. held one knight's fee in Moteland, 1173 ... 　 Gervas de Hornicote amerced for a⊤ breach of the Forest Laws 1198. Paid scutage 1st, 5th, 6th, and 9th John, ob. 1207.

Roger de Carminow,⊤.. witnessed a charter 1220, relating to Tre-nant. 　 Robert de Tintaioel gave 40 marks to have the whole of the inheritance which was Gervase de Hornicote's his father, 1207. In 1211 he held 12 fees of Roger de Mandeville and paid scutage, as he did again 1214 and 1223, ob. 1224.

Robert de Carminow held 15 librates⊤.. of land in Cornwall and of full age and not made a knight. Witnessed a charter 1235. 　 Gervas de Hornicote, *alias* Tintaioel,⊤ held 5 fees in Hornicote and Tin-taioel 1235 (Testa de Nevil) and 20th part of one fee in Winianton and Tamerton.

Sir Roger de Carminow,⊤Sara de Hornicote, dau. named in Assize Roll 12th │ and coh. and heir of Edward I. │ her niece Margery. 　 Cenota de Hornicote,⊤.. dau. and coh. 　 Margery, ob. s.p.

John Carmi-now, son and heir, ob. s.p. 　 Roger de Carminow⊤Johanna dau. of .. re-witnessed charters in │ mar. John Arundell. 1300, 1302, ob. 1308. │ Had assignment of (Inq. p.m., 2nd Ed-│ dower from Oliver Car-ward II, No. 73.) │ minow. 　 GervasCar-minow. 　 Maud or Lu mar. Rob Helligan, o 1276

Johanna, ar. illiam ale-rews. 　 ⊤Thomasine. 　 Matilda mar. Sir William Ferrers 　 Elizabeth Pomeroy. 1st wife. 　 ⊤Sir Oliver Carminow,⊤Isolda,═Sibell, aged 30 years on his │ dau. of │ mar. cir. father's death. Paid │ Reginald │ 1335. 40s. of his relief, 10th │ Ferrers. │ 3rd wife. Edw. II. Quit claim-│ 2nd wife. ed 11th Edward III. manors of Wynyan-ton and Kenel to all his sons in successive tail male. 　 Sir John Car-⊤Johanna, d minow, died │ of Sir Jo 1341. Writ │ Glyn. Bur. diem clausit ex-│ church of tremum. Bur. │ Grey Friar in church of │ Bodmin, 1 Grey Friars at Bodmin.

Menaus,═Thomasine. ob. s.p. Richard.

Eliza-⊤Sir John eth. │ Arundell │ of Lan-│ herne. 　 John Tre-⊤Matilda. varthian. 　 Sir Roger Carminow⊤Elizabeth, dau. of son and heir. Died │ Sir William Botreaux. on Sunday next after │ (See Hist. of Trigg, the feast of the An-│ Vol. 1, p.640), named nunc. B.V.M. 1348. │ as relict of Roger Minister's Accts. │ 1354. (De Banco Duchy of Cornw. │ Roll, 27th Edward │ III, Trin.) 　 Mr. Thomas Carmynow. Rector of Daugan, 1349 to 1361. 　 John. Richard. 　 Margaret, mar. John Beaupre. ob. s.p.

Roger Carminow, ob. s.p. and v.p.

Sir John Arundell of⊤Joan, dau. of Sir Lanherne. │ William Lustock. 　 John Trevarthian, one of the heirs of Johanna Carminow, aged 36 years 1396. 　 Sir Thomas Carminow.⊤Elizabeth, dau. of Sir Bur. in Grey Friars Bod-│ Ralph Beaupre, living min 1369. (See Hist. of │ 1357. (Charter 31st Trigg, Vol. 1, p. 189.) │ Edward III.)

A   B

CARMINOW, HORNICOTE, BLOYOU, AND TINTEN.

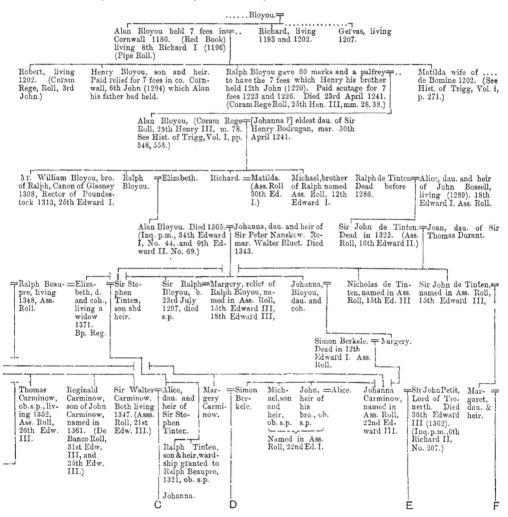

PEDIGREE OF THE FAMILIES OF CARMINO

A   **B**

John Arundell of Lanherne, one of the heirs of Johanna Carminow. Aged 28 years in 1396. Died on Tuesday next after the feast of the Epiphany, 1442-3. (Inq. p.m., 20th Henry VI, No.36.)

Katherine, dau. of .. assigned dower as Widow of Thomas. (Inq. p.m., 13th Rich. II, No.105.) = Thomas Carminow = Jane, dau. son and heir. Died of ...... on Saturday next Whales. after the feast of brew. St. Martin (11th Nov.) Inq. p.m., 12th Richard II. No. 11.

Katherine, dau. and coh. of Sir William Champernon, relict of (Sir Walter?) Wodeland. 14th June 1572. (De Banco Roll 17th Richard II, Hil. m. 244d.) Then dead s.p. = Sir Ralph Carminow, son and heir. Died 9th Oct. 1386. His brother William his heir, aged 30 years. Inq. p.m., 10th Richard II, No. 11. Will proved at Lambeth, 31st Jan. 1386-7, ob. s.p. = Alice, dau. of .. Re-mar. Sir John Rodeney, ob. 1400, and afterwards Sir Wm. Bonville, ob. 1408. She died Wednesday next after the feast of the Annunc. of the B.V.M., 1425. (Inq.p.m.,4thHenry VI, Nos. 24 and 28. See Hist. of Trigg, Vol. i, p. 394*.)

Alice named in her father's will but died before him.

Johanna, dau. and heir. Aged 3 years on her father's death. Died 20th Feb. 1396, Inq. p.m., 19th Richard II, No.15. John Arundell and John Trevarthean nearest heirs.

John Carminow, son and heir. Aged 23 years on his father's death. Had grant of the Manor of Polrode from Alice, wife of Sir William Bonville. Died 26th July 1420. (Inq. p.m., 8th Henry V, No. 99.) = Alice, dau. of Sir John Dynham.

Thomas Carminow, aged 40 years 1420. Heir of his nephew John Carminow. Died Wednesday next before Christmas 1442. (Inq. p.m., 21st Henry VI, No. 46.) = Johanna, dau. of Otho, relict of Otho Trevarthian. Died 7th Aug. 1440. (Inq. p.m., 19th Henry VI, No. 37. See Hist. of Trigg, Vol. i, p. 555.)

John Carminow, son and heir, a ward of John Arundell of Trerice, Knt. Died 6th May 1420. s.p. (Inq. p.m., 8th Henry V, No. 99.) = Johanna, dau. of John Arundell of Trerice. Re-mar. Thomas Bodulgate. Died 17th March 1453-4. (Inq. p.m., 33rd Henry VI, No. 10.)

Margaret, dau. and coh. Aged 20 years on her father's death. Mar. Hugh Courtenay.

Jane, dau. and coh. Aged 15 years on her father's death. Mar. Sir Thomas Carew, Baron Carew (Inq. p.m., 21st Henry VI). Remar. Halnathan Mauleverer. (Ass. Roll, Manor of Helston in Trigg, 9th Edward IV.)

Thomas Carminow.

Jane Carminow, mar. 1st.John Pentyre,2ndly Humphry Calwodely of Helland. Died 28th Sept. 1537. (Inq.p.m., 29th and 30th Henry VIII,No.12. See Hist. of Trigg, Vol. ii, pp. 38, 41.)

Elizabeth, mar. John Bere of.Pengelly. (See.Hist. of Trigg,Vol. i, p. 311.)

Catherine, mar. Humphry Battyn of Dunsland.

Elizabeth, mar. Nicholas Opye of Bodmin. See brass in St. Mawer Church. (Hist. of Trigg, Vol. iii, Plate lviii.)

Isabella, mar. John Viell of Trevorder. Died 7th April 1546. (Inq. p.m., 37th and 38th Henry VIII, No. 4 Exchq.)

Phillippa, mar. 1st John Penfound, and 2ndly. Peter Bevill.

Thomas Carminow of the Privy Chamber to King Henry VIII. Made Constable of Restormel Castle, and held divers other offices. (Inq. p.m., 1st Edward VI, Vol. i, p. 41). Will dated 16th Feb. 1528. Proved 15th May 1529. (Jenkyn 7). P.C.C. To be buried in the Church of Grey Friars at Bodmin. His wife Elizabeth, executrix. = Elizabeth, dau. of .... Chesman of co. Middlesex. Executrix to her husband's will. Remar. Edward Clyker,before 1545 (Asses.Roll,Manor of Restormel, 37th Henry VIII.)

Walter Carminow, 3rd son, named in father's will. His uncle John settled upon him the manor of Tregarrick in tail male. (Ped. Fin. 34th Henry VIII, Easter.)

Nicholas Carminow, 2nd son, upon whom his uncle John settled the manor of Tregarrick in remainder. (Ped. Fin. 34th Henry VIII, Easter.) Bur.[2] 1569. = ...

John Carminow of Fentongollen, son and heir, aged 27, 1547. (Inq. p.m., 1st Edward VI). Bur.[1] 1592. Will dated 27th January 1587-8. Prov. 17th June 1592. (Harrington, 56). = Margaret, dau of Christopher Tredinnick.

G   **H**

---

[1] At St. Michael Penkevill.   [2] At Lanhydrock.

HORNICOTE, BLOYOU, AND TINTEN—Continued.

C

Sir William Carminow, heir of—Margaret, dau. of ....Kelly, had his brother. Aged 30 years on grant of dower from John Car-his brother's death. Sheriff of minow her son, in Tamerton St. Devon, 14th Richard II. Died Mary. Died 16th Oct. 1419. in 1411. (Inq. p.m., 8th Henry (Inq. p.m., 8th Henry V, No. IV, No. 16.) 57.)

D

Bartholomew Berkele,— living 1309. (Inq. p.m. of Henry Bodrigan, 2nd Edw. II, No. 71.)

E

Michael Petit. =Amic Aged 30 years on heir o his father's death. dau. Born 1332. Tinte

Nicholas Carminow, died=Alice, on Friday, next after the dau. of feast of SS. Philip and (See James 1471 s.p. (Inq. Note, p.m.,11th Edward IV,No. p.66.) 44,) Johanna his niece, wife of Halnathan Mau-leverer, his heir.

Walter=Jane, dau. Carmi- and heir of now. Richard Resprin of Resprin.

Thomas = Margaret, Cheyn- living duit, liv- 1354. ing 1354.

Benedict Ber-=kele, held Cant 1354. Living 40th Edward III (1365.)

John Petit, =N one of the d heirs of John b Cheynduit. E Aged 60 in I 1426. Died a 23rd July Q 1429 C

John Carminow of Fentengollen,=Phillippa, dau. and coh. of son and heir. Will dated 14th Sept. John Trenewith of Fenten-1492. Proved 4th Feb. 1492-3 (Dog-gollen. Died 31st July get 21). Phillippa his wife executrix. 1520. (Inq. p.m., 12th To be buried in Priory Church of Henry VIII, No. 74.) St. Petroc of Bodmin.

John Cheynduit, liv-=Johanna, dau. and ing 1390. heir.

John Cheynduit,=Johanna, relict of died Dec. 1426, Richard Glyvian. s.p. (Inq. p.m.,6th Hen. VI, No. 57.)

John Peti heir. Died 1455. (Inq. Henry VI

John Carminow, aged 40 years in=Margaret, dau. and coh. of Richard 1520. Commr. for Musters for Champernon. Relict of Nicholas Cornwall 1523 (State Papers) Cockworthy, by whom she had a assessed to Subsidy in St. Winnow, daughter Avice, who married John 1525, ob. s.p. Conveyed his Trevelyan of Nettlecomb, co. lands to his brother Nicholas and Somerset. Margaret died 21st his nephew Nicholas, (Inq. p.m. 1st April 1529, and the aforesaid Edward VI, No. 41). Died 31st Mar. Avice was found to be her heir, 1547, s.p. Will dated 1st Jan. 1545, and aged 40 years. (Inq. p.m., 21st proved 5th Feb. 1554 (Moore, 19). Henry VIII, No. 159.) To be buried in the Church of St. Michael Penkevil.

Nicholas Carminow, had grant=Katherine, 2 of the manor of Trenewith from coh. of John mother, 19th Mar. 1519-20, and of Devon. I of the manor of Trewethynick from Feb. 1557-8. his brother John, 21st April 1532. 30th Henry Comm. of Musters Cornwall 1523. 61. (State Papers). Died 7th Jan. 1557-8. (Inq. p.m., 30th Henry VIII, No. 56.)

Elizabeth, aged Jane, 2nd Phillippa, 3rd dau. Aged 21 years in 1538, dau., ob. 19 years in 1538. Mar. mar. Nicholas s.p Hugh Boscawen, and 2ndly Herle of Tre- James Trewinard. (Inq. nouth. Inq. 30th p.m., 30th Henry VIII.) Henry VIII.

[1] At St. Michael Penkevil.

X

PEDIGREE OF THE FAMILIES OF CARMINOW, HORNICOTE, BLOYOU; AND TINTEN—Continued.

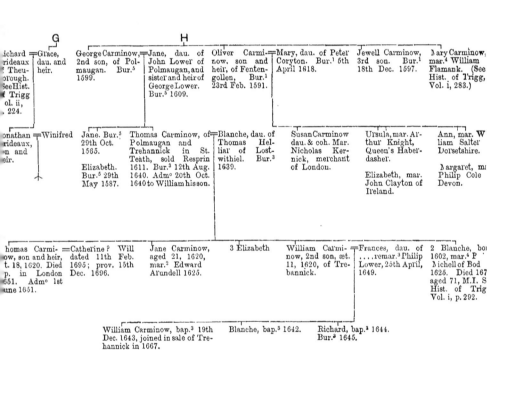

G

H

...ichard =Grace, .rideaux dau. and
Theu- heir.
.orough.
SeeHist.
f Trigg
ol. ii,
, 224.

George Carminow,=Jane, dau. of
2nd son, of Pol- | John Lower of
maugan. Bur.⁵ | Polmaugan, and
1599. | sister and heir of
| George Lower.
| Bur.⁵ 1609.

Oliver Carmi-=Mary, dau. of Peter
now, son and | Coryton. Bur.¹ 5th
heir, of Fenten- | April 1618.
gollen, Bur.¹
23rd Feb. 1591.

Jewell Carminow,
3rd son. Bur.¹
18th Dec. 1597.

Mary Carminow,
mar.⁴ William
Flamank. (See
Hist. of Trigg,
Vol. i, 283.)

onathan =Winifred
.rideaux,
n and
eir.

Jane. Bur.⁵
29th Oct.
1565.

Elizabeth.
Bur.⁵ 29th
May 1587.

Thomas Carminow, of=Blanche, dau. of
Polmaugan and | Thomas Hel-
Trehannick in St. | liar of Lost-
Teath, sold Resprin | withiel. Bur.³
1611. Bur.³ 12th Aug. | 1639.
1640. Adm° 20th Oct.
1640 to William his son.

Susan Carminow
dau. & coh. Mar.
Nicholas Ker-
nick, merchant
of London.

Ursula, mar. Ar-
thur Knight,
Queen's Haber-
dasher.

Elizabeth, mar.
John Clayton of
Ireland.

Ann, mar. W
liam Salter
Dorsetshire.

Margaret, m
Philip Cole
Devon.

homas Carmi- =Catherine ? Will
ow, son and heir, | dated 11th Feb.
t. 18, 1620. Died | 1695; prov. 15th
p. in London Dec. 1696.
651. Adm° 1st
une 1651.

Jane Carminow,
aged 21, 1620,
mar.² Edward
Arundell 1625.

3 Elizabeth

William Carmi-=Frances, dau. of
now, 2nd son, æt. | .....remar.³ Philip
11, 1620, of Tre- | Lower, 25th April,
bannick. | 1649.

2 Blanche, bo
1602, mar.⁴ P
Michell of Bod
1625. Died 167
aged 71, M.I. S
Hist. of Trig
Vol. i, p. 292.

William Carminow, bap.³ 19th
Dec. 1643, joined in sale of Trehannick in 1667.

Blanche, bap.³ 1642.

Richard, bap.³ 1644.
Bur.³ 1645.

¹ At St. Michael Penkevill.   ² At St. Breoke.   ³ At St. Teath.   ⁴ At St. Winnow.   ⁵ At Lanhydrock

TAVERNER.

The name of Taverner is of considerable antiquity in the county of Cornwall. In 1294 Roger le Taverner gave half a mark for a writ of trespass, and in 1306 Nicholas le Taverner gave a like sum for a similar writ.[1] In 1313 Michael le Taverner was, with many others, a defendant in an assize of novel disseizin upon the complaint of Stephen de Trewent of Merchants Goduna concerning his free tenement in Goduna, in which the said Stephen was unsuccessful.[2] Amadis le Taverner was burgess in Parliament for Bodmin in 1317 and 1318.[3] In 1334 an assize of view of recognizance was held to inquire if Nicholas le Taverner of Porthenys and Margaret his wife and Benedict Noght of Portheneys and Johanna his wife had unjustly disseized Robert le Venour of his free tenement in Portheneys. Nicholas and the others, in defence, pleaded that a certain Robert le Venour married Joanna, by whom he had a son Henry and two daughters, the aforesaid Margaret and Johanna. Afterwards the said Johanna, the wife, died and the said Robert married a certain Marina, by whom he had the aforesaid Richard, so that, it was pleaded, on the death of Robert the aforesaid Richard was seized of the said messuages, and that as he died seized thereof s.p. the aforesaid Margaret and Johanna entered as sisters and heirs of the said Henry, upon whom the aforesaid son of Marina, not being of the entire blood, intruded himself, and the same Margaret and Johanna removed him as was lawful for them to do.[4] In 1346 Roger Taverner was one of the pledges for Thomas Maenhir in a suit of assize of novel disseizin against Walter Dyer of Bodmin respecting tenements there and at Bodiniel.[5] Roger Taverner was burgess in Parliament for Launceston in 1553.[6]

John Taverner in 1435 held Trelightes of the manor of Roscarrockmeur (Hist. of Trigg, Vol. i, 525) and John Taverner, probably his descendant, was assessed to the subsidy in St. Kew upon goods of the value of 20 marks in 1521-3.[7] It was probably John, son of this John, who married Johanna the daughter and coheir of Peter Dawnand, and thereupon settled in St. Teath where he was assessed to the subsidy upon lands of the value of 40s. per annum in 1558.[8] Among the lands he acquired by this marriage was Trevylly, and there is extant a petition to Nicholas Bacon, Lord Keeper of the Great Seal, in which "John Tavorner of St. Teath, Gent., complains " that whereas he was seized of a good profit and a sure estate of a messuage and twenty acres of land, twenty acres of meadow and pasture, and twenty acres of furze and heath in Trevyllie in the parish of St. Teath in the right of one Jobane his wife, the daughter and heir of Peter Dawnand, Gent.,

[1] Rot. Fin., 33rd and 34th Edward I.

[2] Assize Roll, 7th Edward II, 2 $\frac{N}{15}$ 6. m. 2.

[3] See Hist. of Trigg, Vol. i, p. 240.

[4] Assize Roll, 8th Edward III 2 $\frac{N}{19}$ 7, m. 12.

[5] Assize Roll 20th Edward III, 2 $\frac{N}{16}$ 6 m. 8 d.

[6] C. S. Gilbert, Hist. Cornwall, Vol. ii, p. 513.

[7] Sub. Roll, Hist. of Trigg, Vol. ii, p. 276.

[8] Sub. Roll, 1st Elizabeth $\frac{8}{218}$

X²

deceased," and had been seized and received the profits for about twenty years, about four years previously one Thomas Thomlin and Henry Bathe at the instigation of one William Courtney, Gent., had entered into the premises and had dispossessed him (the said John); and there finding divers writings and muniments had carried away the same, &c.; and he prays that the said Thomas and Henry may be summoned to appear before the Lord Keeper to answer, as right doth require.[1] We are unable to trace any further proceedings, but John Taverner must have recovered the estate, for it was held by the family long subsequently. In 1571, John Tavernor was again assessed to the subsidy in St. Teath.[2] By his wife Johanna he would seem to have had a son Thomas, and three daughters.

Thomasine the other daughter and coheir of Peter Dawnand married William Taverner, probably a brother of the last mentioned John.[3] In 1588, William Taverner and Thomasine his wife suffered a fine in a moiety of the manor of Dawnandussell and other Dawnand lands to Richard Taverner,[4] who was, we think, their son, and two years afterwards another fine was levied in which John Dagge and William Triplett were querists, and Richard Taverner, Gent., and Thomas Taverner, Gent., deforciants, whereby one messuage in St. Teath Churchtown was settled upon the said Thomas and the heirs male of his body, in default of such issue remainder to the aforesaid Richard and his heirs.[5] In 1594, both Richard Taverner and William Taverner were assessed to the subsidy upon lands in St. Teath, the former at £3, and the latter at 40s. per annum.[6] In 1606, Richard Taverner, Gent., was one of the parties to the alienation to Stephen Toker of certain lands in the parishes of Helland and St. Endellion.[7]

Richard Taverner died in 1613, leaving a daughter and heir named Margaret, who, in 1603, married Moses Langford of Bratton Clovelly, Co. Devon, who by her (as well as other children) had a son and heir Taverner Langford,[8] who inherited her estates in St. Teath, and was assessed to the subsidy upon lands in that parish in 1641 at £4 per annum,[9] as his grandfather, Richard Taverner, had been upon £3 in 1594. He married first, at St. Teath, in 1633, Grace daughter of ...... Nicolls, who died two years afterwards, and was buried at Bratton Clovelly, leaving a son John. (See Ped., p. 78.) His second wife's name was Mary, by whom he had several children baptized at St. Teath between 1640 and 1650.[10]

Thomas Taverner was assessed to the subsidy in St. Teath in 1622,[11] upon lands at 20s. He died in 1628, and was succeeded by his son William, who, in 1641, was assessed upon lands at £3,[12] whilst John Taverner was an agistment holder.[13] In 1652 a

---

[1] Miscellaneous Chancery Proceedings, Part 20. This document is not dated, but it must have been presented sometime between 1558 and 1579, during which period Sir Nicholas Bacon held the Great Seal.

[2] Sub. Roll, 13th Elizabeth $\frac{88}{225}$

[3] See Hist. of Trigg, Vol. i, p. 525.

[4] Pedes Finium, 30th Elizabeth, Trinity.

[5] Ibid. 32nd Elizabeth, Trinity.

[6] Subsidy Roll, 36th Elizabeth $\frac{88}{253}$

[7] Pedes Finium, 3rd James, Hilary.

[8] See Pedigree of Langford, post, p. 78.

[9] Subsidy Roll, 17th Charles $\frac{89}{334}$

[10] Parish Registers.

[11] Sub. Roll, 20th James $\frac{88}{289}$

[12] Ibid, 17th Charles $\frac{89}{334}$

[13] Ibid $\frac{89}{338}$

fine was levied in which Thomas Taverner was plaintiff, and William Taverner (son of Thomas) and Grace his wife, defendants, whereby one messuage in Trevelly which William and Grace held during the life of Grace, with reversion to Taverner Langford and his heirs, was granted by the said William and Grace to the said Thomas for the term of seventy years, if the said Grace so long should live.[1]

The family continued at Trevelly until 1742, when it became extinct in the male line upon the death of Thomas Taverner, great grandson of the abovementioned William, and wholly extinct on the death of his only surviving sister Ann Taverner in 1774.

ARMS: According to C. S. Gilbert this family bore for arms: Argent a bend lozengy; in the sinister quarter a torteaux. As, however, these arms were granted in 1575, and confirmed in 1604, to a family of the same name in Essex and Kent, the right of the Taverners of St. Teath to them is very questionable.

[1] Pedes Finium, 1652, Michs.

PEDIGREE OF TAVERNER OF ST. TEATH.

John Taverner, living 1435. (See Hist. of Trigg, Vol. i, fo. 525.

John Taverner, living 1521

Peter Dawnand, see ante p. 53

John Taverner of St. Teath, assessed to the subsidy 1558. Bur[1]. 3rd Dec. 1586. Admo. at Archd. Court of Cornw. 9th May 1587, Act. lost. =Johanna, dau. and heir of Peter Dawnand. Bur.[1] 27th Jan. 1580.*

William Taverner living 1588 Son and heir. Bur.[1] 25th July 1605. Will prov. Archd. Court 8th July 1606. =Thomasine, dau. and coheir of Peter Dawnand, bur.[1] 28th Feb. 1594.

Thomas Taverner,=.. living 1590. Ped. Finium, 30th Eliz. Bur.[1] 11th March 1628.

Catherine, bap. 19th Dec. 1567. Bur. at Bodmin 1596?

Ann bur. 31st May 1581

Joanna, bur. 1588.

Richard Taverner, living 1588. Ped. Fin., 2nd April 1613. Will dated 23rd Dec. 1608, Prov. 28th May 1613. Archd. Cornwall. =Jane. 30th Eliz., Trinity. Bur.,[1]

William Taverner of St. Teath bap. 22nd Nov. 1588. Ass. to subsidy 1641. Bur.[1] 18th Dec. 1658. =Grace, dau. of .. May, mar. March 1626, Will prov. Archd. Cornwall 18 April 1670 (missing)

Catherine, bap. 27th Nov. 1598.

Oliver, bur. 19th Dec. 1592.

Margaret, dau. and heir, bap.[1] 1589, mar.[1] 13th Sept. 1603. =Moses Langford of Bratton Clovelly. See Pedigree next page.

William, bap.[1] 27th Nov. 1631, bur.[1] 1632.

Joane, bap.[1] 1628.

Margaret, bap.[1] 5th April 1634, mar.[2] 8th June, 1654, Wm. Hockin of Michaelstow,

Thomas Taverner, bur.[1] 26th February 1704-5. =Ann, dau. of .. Pearse, mar. 22nd June, 1652, bur.[1] 2nd April 1698.

William Taverner, bap.[1] 4th Sep. 1653, bur. 29th Nov. 1690. =Phillippa, dau. of Nicholas Philipps, mar.[1] 28th April 1681, bur.[1] 1691.

Grace, bap.[1] 4th Dec. 1662.

Jane, bap.[1] 25th Nov. 1665, bur.[1] 27th June 1693.

Ann, bap.[1] 5th April, 1668, bur.[1] 8th Aug. 1669.

Thomas Taverner, bap.[1] 9th March 1681, bur.[1] 1742, s.p.

John Taverner, bap.[1] 13th March 1683, bur.[1] 8th July 1687.

Phillippa, bap.[1] 8th July 1687, bur.[1] 20th Oct. 1702.

Ann, bap.[1] 3rd March 1689, bur.[1] 1774.

[1] At St. Teath.   [2] At Michaelstow.

* A will of Joane Taverner was proved in the Archdeaconry Court of Cornwall, 12th December 1604, but is lost.

PEDIGREE OF THE FAMILY OF LANGFORD.

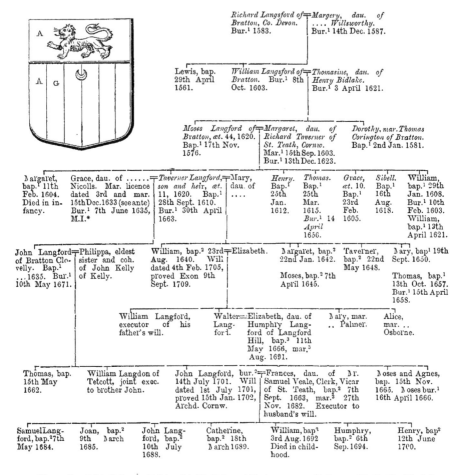

Richard Langsford of *=* Margery, dau. of
Bratton, Co. Devon. | .... Willsworthy.
Bur.[1] 1583. | Bur.[1] 14th Dec. 1587.

Lewis, bap. | William Langsford of *=* Thomasine, dau. of
29th April | Bratton. Bur.[1] 8th | Henry Bidlake.
1561. | Oct. 1603. | Bur.[1] 3 April 1621.

Moses Langford of *=* Margaret, dau. of | Dorothy, mar. Thomas
Bratton, æt. 44, 1620. | Richard Taverner of | Corington of Bratton.
Bap.[1] 17th Nov. | St. Teath, Cornw. | Bap.[1] 2nd Jan. 1581.
1576. | Mar.[1] 15th Sep. 1603. |
| Bur.[1] 13th Dec. 1623. |

Margaret,	Grace, dau. of ...... *=* Taverner Langford, *=* Mary,	Henry.	Thomas.	Grace,	Sibell.	William,
bap.[1] 11th	Nicolls. Mar. licence	son and heir, æt.	dau. of	Bap.[1]	Bap.[1]	æt. 10.	Bap.[1]	bap.[1] 29th
Feb. 1604.	dated 3rd and mar.	11, 1620. Bap.[1]	....	25th	25th	Bap.[1]	16th	Jan. 1608.
Died in in-	15th Dec. 1633 (see ante)	28th Sept. 1610.		Jan.	Mar.	23rd	Aug.	Bur.[1] 10th
fancy.	Bur.[1] 7th June 1635,	Bur.[1] 30th April		1612.	1615.	Feb.	1618.	Feb. 1603.
	M.I.*	1663.			Bur.[1] 14	1605.		William,
					April			bap.[1] 13th
					1656.			April 1621.

John Langford *=* Philippa, eldest	William, bap.[2] 23rd *=* Elizabeth.	Margaret, bap.[2]	Taverner,	Mary, bap[1] 19th
of Bratton Clo-	sister and coh.	Aug. 1640. Will	22nd Jan. 1642.	bap.[2] 22nd	Sept. 1650.
velly. Bap.[1]	of John Kelly	dated 4th Feb. 1705,		May 1648.	
...1635. Bur.[1]	of Kelly.	proved Exon 9th	Moses, bap.[2] 7th		Thomas, bap.[1]
10th May 1671.		Sept. 1709.	April 1645.		13th Oct. 1657.
					Bur.[1] 15th April
					1658.

William Langford,	Walter *=* Elizabeth, dau. of	Mary, mar.	Alice,
executor of his	Lang-	Humphry Lang-	.. Palmer.	mar. ...
father's will.	ford.	ford of Langford		Osborne.
		Hill, bap.[3] 11th		
		May 1666, mar.[3]		
		Aug. 1691.		

Thomas, bap.	William Langdon of	John Langford,	bur.[2] *=* Frances, dau. of	Mr.	Moses and Agnes,
15th May	Tetcott, joint exec.	14th July 1701.	Will	Samuel Veale, Clerk, Vicar	bap. 15th Nov.
1662.	to brother John.	dated 1st July 1701,	of St. Teath, bap.[2] 7th	1665. Moses bur.[1]
		proved 15th Jan. 1702,	Sept. 1663, mar.[2] 27th	16th April 1666.
		Archd. Cornw.	Nov. 1682. Executor to	
			husband's will.	

SamuelLang-	Joan, bap.[2]	John Lang-	Catherine,	William, bap[3]	Humphry,	Henry, bap[2]
ford, bap.[2] 7th	9th March	ford, bap.[2]	bap.[2] 18th	3rd Aug. 1692.	bap.[2] 6th	12th June
May 1684.	1685.	10th July	March 1689.	Died in child-	Sep. 1694.	1700.
		1688.		hood.		

The portion of this Pedigree which is printed in *italics* and the Arms agree with the record in the Herald's College.

Plate LIV.

VIEW OF TEMPLE CHAPEL.

from a Photograph by

REV. J C PARKYN OF BLISLAND

J Ferguson, lith.

Machre & Macdonald, Lith^{rs} to the Queen, London.

FAMILY OF DAGGE.

The family of Dagge was settled in St. Teath at a very early period. Roger Dageys was assessed to the subsidy there in 1327.[1] Thence the family migrated to St. Kew and Endellion. A branch settled in Bodmin and flourished there and at Fowey.[2] John Dagge the third son of Stephen Dagge of Trewigget, in St. Kew, married the daughter and heir of [John?] Treffry of St. Teath, and settled himself in that parish, where he founded the branch of which we now write. In 1558 he was assessed to the subsidy in St. Teath upon goods of the value of £8.[3] He would appear to have left several children, though, having been baptized before the parish registers commence, we have no direct evidence of their birth. Peter Dagge, who would seem to have been the eldest son, was assessed to the subsidy in 1594 upon goods of the value of £5, as he was again upon £8 in 1600; whilst John Dagge, upon the former of these levies, was assessed upon £3.[4]

In 1590 John Dagge was a party to the settlement of a tenement in St. Teath Church Town by Richard Taverner upon Thomas Taverner and the heirs male of his body.[5] And in 1623 John Dagge and Dorothy his wife were parties to the conveyance of Great Hendra in St. Teath,[6] to John Mohun, Esq. We have been unable to identify this John and Dorothy, or to find a place for them in the pedigree, but " Mrs. Dorothy Dagge, widow, was buried" at St. Teath "on 8th April 1667."[7] In 1628 John Dagge, Gent., Peter Dagge, Gent., and Isabella his wife, and John Dagge, Junr., Gent., suffered a fine in Treburgett to Eusebius Orchard.[8] John Dagge, the elder, just mentioned, died in 1645 s.p., as did John Dagge, Junr., in 1683, administration of whose effects was granted to his brother of the same name.

On 20th November 1666, John Nicholls of Trewane, Esq., on the surrender of two former leases and deeds of assignment, one of which was granted by John Nicholls, father of the said John Nicholls, to Richard Dagge for a term of ninety-nine years, if the said Richard Dagge and John Dagge should so long live; and the other, in reversion, for a like term, if Christian Dagge the now wife[9] of the said John Dagge should so long live, granted to the said John Dagge, described as John Dagge, the elder, of Treveighan, Gent., all that messuage known as Treveighan if the said John Dagge and Christian his wife, and John Dagge their son, should so long live.

John Dagge the son died in 1687, when this branch of the family would seem to have become extinct.

[1] Sub. Roll, 1st Edward III.

[2] See Hist. of Trigg, Vol. i, p. 295, ii, 178, and seq.

[3] Sub. Roll, 1st Elizabeth.

[4] Subsidy Rolls, 36th and 42nd Elizabeth $\frac{88}{253-265}$

[5] Ped. Fin , 32nd Elizabeth, Trinity.

[6] Ibid. 21st James, Easter.

[7] Parish Registers.

[8] Ped. Fin., 4th Charles, Michs.

[9] This would seem to imply that John had another wife previous to Christian. The Parish Registers would indicate that he had one or two after her death, for we find that " Mary the wife of John Dagge was buried " in 1673; and in 1684, appears the entry of the burial of another " Mary the wife of John Dagge." We have done our best in the compilation of the annexed Pedigree, and believe that it, upon the whole, is accurate, but the evidence of identity is somewhat defective.

PEDIGREE OF DAGGE.

John Dagge of St. Teath ⊤ ....dau. and heir of
assessed to subsidy there | [John [2]] Treffry of
1558. Bur.[1] 19th January | St. Teath. (Ped. Hist.
1564. | of Trigg, Vol. i, p. 296.)

Peter Dagge of St. ⊤ Jane, dau. of ....   Richard,   John Dagge, ⊤ Catherine ?   Thomasine, mar.[1]
Teath assess. to sub. | Taverner, mar.[1]   bur.[1]   assess. to sub. | Bur.[1] 1623.   Wm. Roche.
1594-1600. Bur.[1] | 11th Nov. 1571.   1597.   1594. Bur.[1]
1628. | Bur.[1] 1622.   1605.

Cather-	John Dagge,	Gonnett,	Peter ⊤ Isabella,	Marga-	John ⊤ Gunnett,	Wil- ⊤	Richard, ⊤ Eliza-	Thomas,
ine, bap.[1]	bap.[1] 1574, of	bap.[1]	Dagge,	dau. of . .	ret, bap.[4]	Dagge,	dau. of . .	liam,	bap.[1]	beth,	bap.[1]
1572,	Seffenton. ass.	1577,	bap.[1]	Nicholls,	1585,	of Tre-	Browne,	bap.[1]	1596,	dau. of	1598.
mar.[1] ..	to subsidy	mar.[1]	1579,	mar.[1]	bur.[1]	kee,	mar.[1]	1592.	bur.[1]	Slog-
Penhel-	1622, 1629 &	1600,	assess.	1603.	1612.	bap.[1]	1617.	Bur.[1]	18th	gett,
lick.	1641. Will	John	to sub.	Bur.		1590,		1665.	July	mar.[1]
	dated 30th	Rawling	1622.	1651.		bur.[1]			1597.	1639.
	Mar. Prob.	alias	Bur.[1]			1619.				
	2nd May 1645	Bennett.	1653.							
	Archd.Cornw,	⊤								
	ob. s.p.									

John Dagge, ⊤ Eliza-	Thomas- ⊤	Peter ⊤	Margaret,[1]	William,	John Dagge ⊤ Christian.	William, ⊤ Elizabeth,
bap.[1] 1604, of	beth,	Dagge,	Dagge	bap. 1608.	bap.[1]	adm[rd] to	Bur.[1] 1670.	bp.[1] 1627	of Blake,
Treveighan in	bur.[1]	bap.[1] 1606.	bap.[1]		1617.	brother			1650.
St. Teath.	1683.	Bur.[1] 1675.	1611,	Catherine,		JohnDagge			
Bur.[1] 1683.			assess.	bap.[1] 1614.		Bur.[1] 1685.			
Adm° to bro.			of sub.						
John Dagge			1672.	Isabel,bap.[1]					
18th January				1619.					
1683, Archd.									
Cornw.				Grace,bap.[1]					
				1624, mar.[1]					
				1656 Geo.					
				Brent.					

James, bur.	John Dagge, bap.	John Dagge, bap.	Ann, bap.[1] 1649,	Elizabeth, bap.[1]
1653.	1651, bur.[1] 1687.	1649, bur.[1] 22nd	mar.[1] 1673 Wm.	1653, bur.[1] 1686.
		May 1670.	Phillips.	

---

[1] At St. Teath.   [2] Assessed to subsidy in St. Teath 1543. (See Appendix iii, p. 84.)

APPENDIX 1.

Parochia Sancte Tethe.

De Willelmo Raauf	-	-	vj*d*	
De Bartholomeo Pardoner	-	-	vj*d*	
De Rogero Droym	-	-	ix*d*	
De Stephane Symond	-	-	vj*d*	
De Rogero Cabba	-	-	vj*d*	
De Johanne Terry	-	-	xij*d*	
De Willelmo Kirkeby	-	-	xij*d*	
De Willelmo Mark	-	-	ix*d*	
De Xpofero Denant	-	-	vj*d*	
De Osberto de Talgragen	-	-	xij*d*	
De Nicholao Osbert	-	-	vj*d*	
De Thomas Dukes	-	-	vj*d*	
De Johanne Dukes	-	-	vj*d*	
De Paulo Reyson	-	-	xij*d*	
De Radulpho Henry	-	-	xij*d*	
De Johanne Lyteman	-	-	ix*d*	
De Henrico Cauel	-	-	ij*s*	
De Radulpho Reson	-	-	vj*d*	
De Michaele Martyn	-	-	ix*d*	
De Margere Kekyl	-	-	ix*d*	
De Ricardo Martyn	-	-	xij*d*	
De Michaele Hoggeskynges	-	-	xij*d*	

De Willelmo Scotta	-	-	xij*d*	
De Willelmo Dollynges	-	-	xij*d*	
De Johanne Hoggeskynges	-	ix*d*	
De Hamone Pancokes	-	-	vj*d*	
De Johanne Waryn	-	-	ix*d*	
De Stephano Pancokes	-	···	xij*d*	
De Willemo Pancokes	-	-	vj*d*	
De Waltero Markes	-	-	xij*d*	
De Radulpho Goybyn	-	-	vj*d*	
De Simone Glysa	-	-	vj*d*	
De Rogero Dageys	-	-	vj*d*	
De Roberto Hordeys	-	-	xij*d*	
De Johanne Jonhyn	-	-	xij*d*	
De Jacobo Jenkyn	-	-	xij*d*	
De Hamone Whita	-	-	xij*d*	
De Ricardo Henry	-	-	ix*d*	
De Willelmo Hamond	-	-	vj*d*	
De Roberto Hamond	-	-	xij*d*	
De Johanne Mouner	-	-	ix*d*	

	De Nicholao Tregartha	vj*d*
Taxatores	De Johanne le Brun	vj*d*
	De Nicholao de Lynewyth	x*d*

APPENDIX II.

Augmentation Office, Miscell. Books, vol. lxxvij, fo. 59.

Tetha.

PAROCHIA DE ⎱
SEYNT TETHA ⎰　 *Valencia Spiritualis possessionis ibidem*

Doctor Tollet valet ibidem in proficuis eiusdem ecclesie per annum　-　　　-　　　- xijli

Mr. Johannes Nane Vicarius ibidem valet per annum　　-　　　-　　　-　　- vjli

Valencia terrarum et tenementarum ibidem.

Willelmus Dawnauat, valet, per annum	cs	Thomas Gilbe ⎫	
Johannes Trehanek - - xxvjs viijd		Arthurus Kemys ⎬ in jure, ux' suorum vs	
Benedictus Tremure - - xxs		Willelmus Carnsuyew ⎭	
Johannes Wattes - - xxs		Willelmus Wynslade - - xs	
Thomas Trelegy - - viijs		Johannes Drew - - iiijs	
Johannes Chapell - - xvjs		Johannes Smyth - - viijs	
Dominus Henricus Courtenay - xiijs iiijd		Johannes Cowlyng - - xxvjs viijd	
Johannes Skuys - - vjli		Christopherus Cok - - xls	
Johannes Rescarek - - xijli		Ricardus Tremayne - - xvjs	
Reginaldus None - - iiijli		Domina de Hastinges - - xs	
Thomas Gilbe - - xs		Johannes Pengelly - - xxxiijs iiijd	
Arthur Kemys - - xs		Prior de Launceston - - vjs viijd	
Nicholaus Cavyll - - xxvjs viijd		Johannes Vyall - - xs	
		Johannes Brode - xijs	

¹ Richard Tollet, collated to the Sub-deancry of Exeter 13th May 1515, which he resigned for the Archdeaconry of Barnstaple, to which he was collated 19th January 1517-18. Died 26th April 1528.

Valencia Bonorum et Catallorum dicta Parochia et de eorum armis.

Thomas Scrivan Capellanus in bonis xl*s*, in stipendio vij *marcas*.

Henricus Wade valet in bonis   c*s*

Johannes Mylward   ,,   vj*li* xiij*s* iiij*d*

Willelmus Kyllyowe   ,,   viij*li* arma pro vno homine

Johannes Trehauek   ,,   c*s* arma pro vno homine

Nicholas Dyer   ,,   nil quia pauper, tenens Willelmi Dawnand

Johannes Tremeere   ,,   vj*li* xiij*s* iiij*d* arma pro vno homine

Benedictus Tremere   ,,   iiij*li*

Johannes Perys senr.   ,,   viij*li* arma pro vno homine

Johannes Hill   ,,   xl*s*

Johannes Lowe   ,,   xvj*li* xiij*s* iiij*d*. arma pro vno homine

Johannes Watte   ,,   xl*s*

Thomas Matthew   ,.   liij*s* iiij*d*

Nicholaus Milward   ,,   xl*s*

Henricus Ronold   ,,   iiij*li*

Johannes Joce   ,,   c*s*

Johannes Herry   ,,   iiij*li* vj*s* viij*d*

Robertus Tom   ,,   xl*s*

Nicholaus Davy   ,,   xl*s*

Radulphus Hawkyn   ,,   iiij*li*

Edwardus Tom   ,,   v *marcas*

Willelmus Cowlyng   ,,   xl*s*

Johannes Donell   ,,   xl*s*

Thomas Cradok   ,,   iiij*li*

Thomas Joce junr.   ,,   v *marcas*

Stephenus Russh   ,,   ii j*li*

Thomas Joce senr. in bonis   v *marcas*

Johannes Tredwen   ,,   xl*s*

Nicholaus Russh   ,,   c*s*

Johannes Edward   ,,   xl*i* arma pro vno homine

Johannes Symon   ,,   xl*s*

Henricus Benet   ,,   iij*li* arma pro vno homine

Thomas Trelege   ,,   viiij*li*

Willelmus Litell Jon   ,,   xl*s*

Edwardus Nicoll   ,,   xl*s*

John Pers de Dalymer   ,,   c*s*

Stephanus Byle   ,,   xl*s*

Willelmus Hamley   ,,   xl*li* arma pro vno homine

Thomas Palmer   ,,   xl*s*

Willelmus Joce   ,,   xl*s*

Thomas Joce junr.   ,,   xl*s*

Henricus Watte   ,,   xx *marcas*

Johannes Treriby   ,,   xl*s*

Robertus Edward   ,,   nil tenens Johannis Rescarek

Johannes Watte   ,,   iiij*li*

Johannes Slogett   ,,   xx*li* arma pro vno homine

Johannes Trebyghan   ,,   v *marcas*, arma pro vno homine

Stephanus Hogge   ,,   xl*s*

Petrus Hillary   ,,   x *marcas*

Thomas Hogge   ,,   c*s*

Johannes Hillary   ,,   xl*s*

Johannes Ronald   ,,   vj*li*

Nomina alieneginorum ibidem et valencia bonorum eorundum.

Johannes Burgyn juner in bonis nil nativus in britonia sub obediencia Regis franciæ.

Y²

APPENDIX III.

SUBSIDY ROLL FOR THE PARISH OF ST. TEATH, 35TH HENRY VIII (1543)—

Parochia de Tethe.

Richard Porquyn	in bonis	xxs Sub.	ijd	John Myllerd	in bonis	vli Sub.	xxd
Stephyn Hyllary	,,	iijli ,,	vjd	John Illary	,,	xxs ,,	ijd
Thomas Syssyly	,,	xxs ,,	ijd	William Hamlye	,,	iiijli ,,	viijd
Nyclas Deer	,,	iiijli ,,	viijd	Richard Hamlye	,,	viijli ,,	ijs viijd
John Pytt	,,	iiijli ,,	viijd	Thomas Josse	,,	iiijli ,,	viijd
John Andro	,,	xxs ,,	ijd	John Symon	,,	xxs ,,	ijd
John Groosse	,,	xls ,,	iiijd	Harry Benytt	,,	iijli ,,	vijd
John Teage	,,	xxs ,,	ijd	Nyclas Benytt	,,	iijli ,,	vjd
Peter Tawnand	,,	vli ,,	xxd	Robert Hockyn	,,	xls ,,	iiijd
William Kyllyowe	,,	ixli ,,	iijs	John Petegrew	,,	xxs ,,	ijd
Thomas Trehenyke	,,	xli ,,	vjs viijd	Harry Goolyn	,,	xxs ,,	ijd
Richard Chapman	,,	xxs ,,	ijd	Nyclas Ranke	,,	xxs ,,	ijd
William Thome	,,	xxs ,,	ijd	Stephyan Rustyne	,,	xls ,,	iiijd
Stephyn Hoge	,,	viijli ,,	ijs viijd	William Rustyne	,,	iiijli ,,	viijd
Richard Millerd	,,	xls ,,	iiijd	Thomas Tregragan	,,	iijli ,,	vjd
Martyn Robye	,,	xxs ,,	ijd	Thomas Tregragan, jun	,,	xxs ,,	ijd
John Treffry	,,	xli ,,	vis viijd	Jamys Treffry	,,	xxs ,,	ijd
John Nycoll	in terris	vli ,,	iijs iiijd	Thomas Edward	,,	vli ,,	xxd
John Hyll	in bonis	iiijli ,,	viijd	John Edward	,,	xijli ,,	viijs
John Thom	,,	iijli ,,	vjd	Robert Edward	,,	vli ,,	xxd
Roger Illary	,,	xxs ,,	ijd	Thomas Davy	,,	vli ,,	xxd
John Loobe	,,	ixli ,,	iijs	John May	,,	xs ,,	ijd
William Loobe	,,	iiijli ,,	viijd	Harry Roche	,,	ixli ,,	iijs
John Wattys	,,	xxs ,,	ijd	John Chapell	,,	xijli ,,	viijs
John Harry	,,	iijli ,,	vjd	Thomas ffynche	,,	xli ,,	vjs viijd
John Tage	,,	vli ,,	xxd	Thomas Hooge	,,	xli ,,	vjs viijd
Roger Heyr	,,	xxs ,,	ijd	John Illarye	,,	iijli ,,	vjd
Thomas Olyver	,,	xls ,,	iiijd	John Illarye, junr.	,,	iijli ,,	vjd
Raffe Hawkyn	,,	xls ,,	iiijd	Thomas Groosse	,,	iiijli ,,	viijd
Nyclas Hawkyn	,,	iijli ,,	vjd	Thomas Lytyll John	,,	xli ,,	vjs viijd
Robert Illary	,,	xls ,,	iiijd	Thamasyn Trehenyke	in terris	xxs ,,	iiijd
John Rawe	,,	xli ,,	vjs viijd	Johanna Wattyt	in bonis	iijli ,,	vjd
Nycoll Symon	,,	xls ,,	iiijd	Johanna Renyll	,,	xxs ,,	ijd
Harry Lynam	,,	ixli ,,	iijs	John Erysche	,,	iiijli ,,	viijd
John Trewenyke	,,	iijli ,,	vjd	Nyclas Tremcere	,,	xxs ,,	ijd
John Hawkyn	,,	xxs ,,	ijd	Le P'or de beate Marie Virgine		iiijli ,,	xvjd
Harry Wattys	,,	iiijli ,,	viijd	Le P'or de Sancti Nyclas		xxs ,,	iiijd
Stephyn Nycoll	,,	iijli ,,	vjd				

Summa hujus parochie ad Subsidium predictum vli viis vid.

PARISH OF TEMPLE.

This little parish, which contains only 843 acres and 25 perches statute measure, is bounded on the north-west and north-east by the parish of Blisland, on the east by St. Neot, on the south-east by Warleggan, and on the south-west by Cardinham. It is situate entirely on the granite formation of precisely the same character as Blisland and St. Breward, and consists, generally, of rough uncultivated land, though there are some grassy pastures. There is no other industry practised by the scanty population than agriculture, chiefly the pasturage of cattle, which are received, for a few weeks in the summer, from the more fertile districts of the county, at a rate per head. Stream tin works have in times past, probably from a very early date, been carried on in the valleys,[1] but have now ceased, though as a new industry has been established in the adjoining parishes in the raising and preparation of *Kaolin*, or China clay, it is probable that it may soon be introduced into Temple.[2] The chief landowners are Lord Robartes, the Messrs. Remfry, the Rev. C. M. Edward-Collins of Trewardale, and Mr. Roger Bate.

The small population has very little varied in number for a considerable period. Hals mentions that when he wrote the parish consisted of only eight tenements and about thirty souls.

The following table will show the number of houses and the population at the several decennia in present century.

		1801	1811	1821	1831	1841	1851	1861	1871
Population		15[3]	18	27	29	37	24	12	34
Houses	Inhabited	2[4]	3	5	5	6	5	3	3
	Uninhabited	1	..	..	..	..	..	..	2
	Building	..	..	..	..	..	..	..	..

[1] One or two of those ancient works known as "Jews' Houses" exist in the parish.

[2] Since this was written we learn that China clay works have been opened in Temple by Mr. F. Parkyn.

[3] The population in 1666 was also 15, as shewn by the Poll Tax, see post, p. 96n.

[4] Occupied by three families.

ASSESSMENTS.

	£	s.	d.
Annual value of real property assessed upon the Parish in 1815	156	0	0
Rated value from County Rate	200	0	0
Rated value from County Rate 1866	176	0	0
Gross estimated rental in 1866 ...	198	0	0
Rateable value in 1866	183	10	0
Gross estimated Rental in 1875 ...	271	5	1
Rateable value in 1875 ...	251	17	6
Parochial Assessments 1875. { Common Charges ...	13	2	4
Police Rate ...	1	18	6
County Rate ...	1	18	6
Land Tax ...	10	0	0
Assessed Taxes ...	not known		
Inhabited House Duty...	nil		
Property and Income Tax assessed upon 1875. Schedule A ...	230	0	0
„ „ „ „ B	217	0	0
D	not known		
E	„		

MEETING HOUSES OF DISSENTERS.

A Meeting House for Bible Christians has recently been erected near the ruined Church. It is calculated to accommodate 100 persons, and there are attached to it eight registered members. It is intended that it shall be vested in Trustees to the uses prescribed in model deed of the Bible Christians' Society.

[1] Poor Rate in 1831 £17 15s.

It is not probable that this little district was taxed separately at the Domesday Survey, and Hals conjectures, probably with correctness, that it was included in Nietestov, which, having been held in the time of King Edward by Bodric, was then held by Odo of the Earl of ᴍoreton, or, possibly, it was held by the Earl with Trebihan (Trebighe), to which it was undoubtedly annexed at a later date.

Temple, with its Chapel, was, until lately, a jurisdiction exempt from the visitation of the Bishop of Exeter, and this circumstance taken in connection with its name and with local tradition would, we think, satisfactorily shew that it was originally a part of the possessions of the Knights Templars; and this is confirmed by the Return of Bishop Grandisson (post). That Order was suppressed through the machinations of the vindictive Philip IV of France, the enemy of the Church, through whose instrumentality, in 1307, a series of charges was brought against the Knights by two ᴍembers of the Order, who had been degraded for their crimes, and were then in prison for other offences. Edward II of England, who had then recently succeeded to the throne, was reluctantly drawn into the persecution, and in 1308 an inquisition was made of all the possessions of the fraternity in England, both in lands and goods. The result of this inquisition is preserved in what are called the Templars' Rolls (2nd and 3rd Edward II) in the Public Record Office. These Rolls enter into very minute details, shewing even the number of poultry upon every estate. It is, however, very singular that no possessions of the Order in the County of Cornwall appear in these records. The fraternity was not actually suppressed until 1314.

Though the kings, both of France and England, seized all the property of the knights, and kept the moveable goods, it was found that they could not retain the landed possessions of the Order, which in England were transferred to the Knights of St. John of Jerusalem, or Hospitallers, in the year 1323,[1] and we find that the Hospitallers held some of the Templars' lands in 1328. They experienced, however, in many instances, great difficulties in obtaining possession. The Lords of the Fees had, in numerous cases, seized the estates, and it was only by process of law they could be recovered, and even as late as 1338, some of the most valuable of the Templars' manors had not been surrendered. Before the last mentioned date they possessed the Preceptory and ᴍanor of Trebighe in Cornwall, as appears from an extent of their lands preserved in the Public Library at ᴍalta, and brought to light by the indefatigable industry of that eminent antiquary, the late Rev. Lambert Larking.[2] It gives not only an extent of the lands, but also the value of the produce and the expenses for the year abovementioned, and is most interesting, moreover, as illustrative of prices at that date. We have, therefore, no hesitation in presenting it to our readers.

---

[1] Statutum de Terris Templariorum, 17th Edward II, Stat. 2.

In 1386, the Prior of the Hospital of St. John of Jerusalem, in England, sued John Stryppa at Haye, and William Lawry, for taking the goods and chattels of the said Prior at Temple, and for beating and insulting his men and servants. They did not appear, and the Sheriff was commanded to attach them. (De Banco Roll, 9th Richard II, Easter, m. 93).

[2] This valuable record was edited for the Camden Society by ᴍr. Larking, and, with an introduction by John ᴍ. Kemble, printed by the Society in 1857.

BAJULIA DE TREBYGHEN.

In Cornubia.

Est ibidem unum mesuagium cum gardino et columbario, et valent per annnm. -	xvj*s.* viij*d.*
Item unum mollendinum aquaticum et valet　-　　　-　　　-　　　-	x*s.* viij*d.*
Item cc acre terre et pasture, pretium acre iij*d.*, valent　-	i*s.*
Item iij acre prati et dimidia, que valent　　-　　　-	iij*s.*[2]
Item de redditu assiso ibidem　　-	xxx*s.*
Et gleba ecclesie Sancti Ivonis　-	iij*d*
Item de gleba Sancti Maderni　-	ix*d.*
Item de gleba Sancti Clare　-　　　-	i marca.
Item de pensione vicarii ecclesie Sancti Maderni　　-　　　-	iiij marce.
Item de ecclesie Sancti Maderni appropriata　-　　-	xliiij marce.
Item de ecclesie de Trebyghen appropriata　-　　　-　　　-	xxviij marce.
Item confraria ibidem solebat valere xxxij marcas, et nunc in presenti vix possunt levari　-　　　-　　　-　　　-　　　-　　　-	xxviij marce.

Summa totalis recepti proficui dicte bajulie cxiij marce iiij*s.* viij*d.*

TREBYGHEN.—Reprise.

In expensis domus, videlicet pro preceptore, confratre suo, et familia
de bajulia, et aliorum supervenientium, causa hospitalitatis, prout
fundatores dicte domus constituerunt, videlicet, in pane furnito xiij.
quarteria frumenti, pretium quarterij iij*s.*, et xx. quarteria siliginis,
pretium quarterij ij*s.* viij*d.*　-　　　-　　　-　　- Summa iij*li.* xij*s.* iiij*d.*

Item in cerevisia bracianda xl. quarteria brasii avenarum, pretium
quarterij. xij*d.*, et xij. quarteria brasij ordei, pretium quarterij ij*s.* viij*d.* Summa lxvj*s.* viij*d.*

Item in carne et pisce pro coquina per septimanam xviij*d.*　-　　-　lxxviij*s.*

Item in robis, mantellis, et aliis necessariis preceptoris et confratris sui　- lxixs. iiij*d.*

Item in stipendio j Capellani ad mensam　-　　　-　　-　xx*s.*

Item in stipendiis familie domus et duorum garciorum preceptoris　-　xxxi*s.* iiij*d.*

Item in prebenda equorum preceptoris et supervenientium per annum xx.
quarteria avenarum, pretium quarterii xij*d.*　-　　　-　　-　xx*s.*

Summa omnium expensarum et solutionum xxx marce x*s.* viij*d.*

Summa Valoris.—Et sic remanent ad solvendum ad Thesaurarium pro
oneribus supportandis　-　　　..　　-　　　- iiij*xx* ij marce vij*s.* iiij*d.*

Nomina Fratrum ｛ Frater Vincentius de Herdwyck, precepto, S.
　　　　　　　　｛ Frater Robertus de Langton, S.[2]

---

[1] The land at Trebyghen (Trebighe) would seem to have been of inferior quality. The price of arable land generally ranged from 6d. to 12d. an acre, and sometimes reached as high as 24d. the acre, but the latter cases are very rare. In some instances, however, we find arable land rated as low as 1d. an acre. Meadow land was of much greater proportionate value, generally 18d. to 24d. per acre, some rising as high as 3s. This would seem to shew that grazing held a disproportionate position to the higher processes of agriculture. The usual method was, however, to let the pasture for grazing at per head, for which about 12d. was paid for an ox, 12d. to 24d. for a cow, and 1d. for a sheep.

[2] The signification of the letter "S" to the names of the Brothers has been a matter of considerable doubt, but J. Mason Kemble has arrived at the conclusion that it must, unquestionably, mean *serviens.* But the *servientes* were of two classes : the noble class of professed, or *servientes armorum,* and the *servientes officio.* The former wore Coat armour and were gentlemen, and were sometimes called *Generosi,* the latter were free servants who attended to the duties of the household. (Introduction to the Knights' Hospitallers in England, p. lxiv.)

In this "extent" Trebyghe is not included among the Templars' lands, nor does it appear from the description that it embraced the manor of Temple. It would seem to us as not improbable that Temple had been concealed, and, from the causes above stated, had not at this date been recovered.

It is said that Henry de Pomerai and Reginald Marsh were considerable benefactors to the Preceptory of Trebigh.[1] It was valued at £60 per annum; but this with Anstey, co. Wilts, in 26th Henry VIII, was valued at £90 1s. 9d., or in the whole, clear, £81 8s. 5d. At the suppression of the confraternity by Act 32nd Henry VIII, cap. 24, all the possessions of the order were transferred to the King, reserving to the lessees all leases which had been granted by the Prior and Brethren.

On 7th July 1524 (16th Henry VIII) the Prior and Confraternity of the Hospital of St. John in England, by indenture under their seal, granted to farm to Sir John Chamond, Knt., and John Welsh all the Preceptory of Trebighe, and all the manor and lordship of Trebigh for the term of forty years from the feast of the Nativity of St. John Baptist preceding, reserving to the Prior and Brethren and their heirs and successors, all the great trees and woods, and the advowsons of all Churches, &c.; and by letters patent, dated 9th March 1550-1, King Edward VI granted the said premises to his servant Robert Gardyner, from the feast of the Nativity of St. John Baptist 1564, when the demise aforesaid to Sir John Chamond and John Welch would expire, for the term of twenty-one years, at the rent of £48 per annum. Philip and Mary, however, upon consultation with Cardinal Pole, determined to restore the Order, and having done so, by letters patent granted to Sir Thomas Tresham and the Hospital of St. John of Jerusalem in England, all the possessions of the old Confraternity then remaining undisposed of, inter alia, the manor, otherwise the preceptory of Trebighe with appurtenances.[2] Soon after the accession of Queen Elizabeth, however, the restored Order was again dissolved, and all their possessions were seized into the Queen's hands, who, by letters patent dated 12th December 1573, granted to Henry Welbye and George Blythe, inter alia, all the manor of Trebyghe with appurtenances, to hold to the said Henry and George, their heirs and assigns for ever of the manor of East Greenwich in common socage at the annual rent of £6 7s.[3] This was for purposes of sale, and by letters patent dated 8th January following, after reciting the beforementioned leases of 7th July 1524, and 9th March 1550-1, in consideration of the sum of £100, the Queen granted to Peter Coryton Esq., and William Hoghen, a lease of the Rectories or Churches of St. Cleer, Madron, and Pensaunte, with all the tithes of corn and grain and hay to the said Churches pertaining, parcel of the preceptory of Trebighe, at the annual rent: for St. Cleer of £8 13s., and for the Rectory of Madron and Pensaunte of £33 per annum, the said Peter Coryton to have, from time to time, " sufficient housebote, hedgebote, fyrebote, ploughbote, and cartebote there."[4]

[1] Tanner, Not. Monast., ed. Nasmith, Cornwall, xxxj.
[2] Rot. Pat., 4th and 5th Philip and Mary, m. 1.
[3] Rot. Origin. 16th Elizabeth, m. 16.
[4] Rot. Pat., 16th Elizabeth, Part 3, m. 13.

Z

In the foregoing records relating to the manor of Trebighe, no specific mention is
made of Temple, but there cannot, we think, be any doubt that it formed a portion of
the possessions of the Preceptory of Trebighe, and was annexed to, or formed a portion
of, the manor. Immediately upon the abovementioned grant of the 12th December, the
manor of Trebighe had passed to John Morley, Gent., and Elizabeth his wife, who in the
following month suffered a fine in the said manor to Peter Coryton, Esq., and William
Coryton, Gent., in which it is described as 12 messuages, 20 gardens, 20 orchards, 2,000
acres of land, 100 acres of meadow, 40 acres of pasture, 200 acres of furze and heath,
300 acres of moor, and 20s. rent in Trebighe, St. Cleere, St. Eve, *Temple*, and Menheniot.[1]
And two years later, the Queen's Minister in Cornwall accounted for £6 7s. received
from Peter Currington, for the farm of all the messuages and demesne lands, &c., parcel
of the manor of Trebighe, granted to Henry Welbie and George Blyth, and for £41 13s.
received of the same person as rent for the farm of all the Preceptory of Trebighe, with
all its members, &c., formerly in the tenure of John Chamond, Knt., and John Welche,
and so demised to Robert Gardyner, for the term of twenty-one years from the feast of
the Nativity of St. John Baptist 1564, the said Robert Gardyner to pay the wages of a
Chaplain to celebrate Divine Offices within the Chapel of the said preceptory.[2] The lease
of the preceptory to Robert Gardyner expired in 1585, but Peter Coryton still continued
to hold the premises as before,[3] and in 1603, the accountant answered for a heriot on the
death of Peter Coryton on the confession of William Coryton his son; but the accountant
notes that no letters patent, or other title, had as yet been produced to the auditor for
Coryton's tenure.[4]

There is, however, some light thrown upon the transaction by certain proceedings in
Chancery in 1569, in which George Julian, *alias* Coriton, complained against Peter Coriton,
concerning a lease for a term of years in the manor of Trebighe, with appurtenances, in
which, reciting the grant by King Edward VI to Robert Gardyner, he alleged that the
said Robert assigned his interest therein to Richard Coryton, Esq., deceased, and the said
Richard being so possessed granted the said lease to the said complainant, unto which
lease the said Peter pretended title. He further alleged that the said Richard Coriton
died intestate, and that Ann Coriton his wife, and mother of the defendant, having
administered to her husband's effects, had granted all her interest in the said lease to the
complainant. The suit was dismissed for trial at common law before Justices of Assize,
and we do not know the result, as touching the lease.[5]

Meanwhile the manor of Trebighe had passed to Henry Killigrew of Wolston, by

---

[1] Pedes Finium, 16th Elizabeth, Hilary.

[2] Minister's Accounts, Cornwall, 18th Elizabeth.

[3] On 4th November 1573, a statement of particulars was prepared for a grant of the manor of Trebighe to
Thomas, Earl of Ormond, in which, after stating that there are seven old oaks of 100 years' growth and more,
which may not be spared for the defence of the house, &c., it is said "also the Queen's Matie giveth the Vicarages
of St. Cleere, Madron, Pensaunce, *and Temple*." The grant is not traced to have been made.

[4] Ibid. 44th Elizabeth and 1st James.

[5] Chancery, Inrolled Decrees, 11th Elizabeth, Part 24, No. 27.

whose daughter and heir, Elizabeth, it was carried in marriage, *inter alia*, to John Wraye, who made Trebighe his residence, and died there on ·10th June 1597,[1] seized, *inter alia*, of the manors of Trebighe and Temple, which he held of the Queen, as of the manor of East Greenwich, by fealty in free and common socage and not in capite, and the annual value beyond reprises was £27 3s. 4d. per annum, and his brother, William Wraye, was found to be his nearest heir, and to be aged forty years and more.[2] In the following year William Wrey, Esq., levied a fine of Ambrose Billett, Esq., and Eleanora his wife, of the annual rent of £100 issuing out of the manor of Trebighe, for which he gave the said Ambrose and Eleanora £1,000.[3] William Wrey of Trebighe was created a baronet in 1628, and in 1632, the Minister accounted for the rent of £6 7s. received from Sir William Wraye, Knight and Baronet, for the farm of the Lordship or Preceptory of Trebighe, parcel of the manor of Trebighe, granted to Henry Welbie and George Bligh (sic), 16th Elizabeth.[4] Since this date the manor of Temple has remained vested in the Wrey family, and now forms parcel of the possessions of Sir Bourchier Wrey, Bart.

THE CHAPEL.

When the Chapel of Temple was founded is unknown. In consequence of the benefice having been an extra parochial donative, exempt from the Bishop's jurisdiction, its name rarely occurs in the Ecclesiastical records. The earliest mention of it, which has fallen under our notice, is in the valuation of Pope Nicholas 1288—1291, in which we find " Capella de Templo " rated at 10s., and it occurs again, in the same form, with the addition of the word " hospital," within a parenthesis in the margin, in the taxation of the Bishops of Lincoln and Winchester in 1294.[5] On 21st March 1331, Bishop Grandisson, at the request of the Prior and Brethren of the Hospital of St. John of Jerusalem in England, relaxed an interdict on " Capella de Templo, in Decanatus de Trigg."[6] This interdict had probably been laid on the Chapel during the period between the tenure of the Knights Templars and the acquisition of their lands by the Knights Hospitallers. On 26th August 1335 the same Bishop certified to King Edward III, that the Prior and Brethren of St. John of Jerusalem then held " Capellam de Temple " " quæ quondam fuit Templariorum, et valet 10s."[7] On the assessment of the " ninths " in 15th Edward III (1341) the valuation of Temple was included with that of Blisland, to which benefice

---

[1] It is stated in a Rental of the Manor of Tresarret, dated in 1598,' that a high rent of 1s. 4d. per annum was payable out of that manor to the *Queen's* manor of Temple. See Hist. of Trigg, vol. ii, p. 491.

[2] Inq. p.m., 39th Elizabeth, Part i, No. 66. [3] Pedes Finium, 40th Elizabeth, Easter.

[4] All the residue of the Preceptory for which a rent of £41 13s. had been paid had now disappeared from the accounts. (Ministers' Accounts, Cornwall, 8th Charles).

[5] Bronescombe's Register. [6] Bishop Grandisson's Register, vol. ii. [7] Ibid.

z²

the Chapel would appear at that time to have been annexed. Of the ninth sheaf, fleece and lamb of the Parish Church of Blyston, with the Chapel of Temple, taxed at £6 10s., and so sold to Hernico (Henrico?) Adam, William Langeston, and Wynam Tyrel.[1] This would be £6 for Bliston and 10s. for Temple. At this rate we find the benefice rated to the subsidy in 1380 as "Capella de Templo," as it was also in 1450. It is not named in Wolsey's Valuation of 1535, nor in the return of Bishop Veysey of the following year, consequently it is not now rated in the King's Books. In a statement of the particulars of the manor of Trebighe, prepared in 1573 for the grant of that manor to Thomas Earl of Ormond, the *Vicarages* of St. Cleer, Madrone, Pensaunce, *and Temple*, are included as pertaining to the manor, with reference to which it should be remarked that Penzance was but a Chapel.

In 1744, the benefice was augmented by a grant of £200 from Queen Anne's Bounty, and thenceforth it became, under the provisions of 1st George I, cap. 10, a perpetual cure and benefice, subject to the visitation and jurisdiction of the Bishop. With this sum was purchased, in 1760, a Tenement in St. Minver called Sparnall's Tenement or Little Weems, containing 12a. 0r. 19p., which is now let at £13 10s., per annum.

The whole of the lands in the parish consists of—

		A.	R.	P.
Arable ...	...	197	1	8
Pasture	...	121	0	1
Common Land ...	...	502	0	14
Wastes[2]...	...	22	3	2
		843	0	25

The whole of which is subject to tithes, except the glebe which contains 1a. 3r. 17p., viz.:

Glebe Meadow ...	...	...	1	3	15
Garden ...				2	
			1	3	17

the tithes of which have been merged in the freehold. The site of the Church and Churchyard contains 2r. 13p. The donative Curate, for the time being, is entitled to all the tithes, which tithes in 1841 were commuted into a rent-charge of £21 per annum, to which should be added the rental of Weems, which makes the total value of the benefice, exclusive of the small glebe, £34 10s. per annum.

Anterior to the year 1744, there are not in the Diocesan Registry any records of the admission of Incumbents to the Cure, but notices are found of the appearance, or non-appearance, of the Curates at the Bishop's Visitations. The earliest notice traced is in the record of Bishop Carey's Visitation, at which time it appears that Sir William Wrey was Patron, and Mark Penkevell was Curate, who appeared and paid the Registrar

---

[1] Inquisitiones Nonarum, fo. 345.

[2] According to Returns recently published by the Tithe Commissioners, the quantity of waste lands in this parish was 211 acres, of which 161 acres were improvable and 50 unimprovable.

twelve pence. He did not appear at the Visitations of 1630 and 1638, but still continued Curate at the latter date. We have no record of another Visitation until 1662, when Philip Leach was Curate, who appeared, as he did also at the Visitation in 1668. In the record of the Visitations of 1671 and 1674, no Curate is named, but in that of 1677, Mr. Roger Chaplaine is mentioned as Curate, who, it is stated, had no licence and was admonished to obtain one. He heeded not, however, the admonition, probably questioning the Bishop's jurisdiction. He appeared again in 1680 and 1683. In 1689, he did not appear, nor did he in 1692, when it is noted that the Bishop excused him as being old. At the Visitation of 1699, the benefice is mentioned as being exempt. Hals names ...... Osborne, Vicar of Liskeard, as Curate of Temple, but as we do not know the exact date to which he refers, it is somewhat uncertain whether he alludes to William Osborne, Vicar of that parish, who died in 1708, or to his son Peter Osborne, who succeeded him at Liskeard, and, in the former case, at Temple also, for he appeared at the Visitations of 1709 and 1712. At the Visitation of 1718, he did not appear. He died in 1723. We have a receipt dated 17th March 1723-4, in which Ann Osborne, probably his relict and administratrix, acknowledged to have "received from Mr. Roger Bate 5s. for tythes to Christmas last for an estate in Temple p'sh."[1] At the Visitation on 26th June 1724, Mr. Stephen Hicks appeared as Curate. In 1728, he did not appear, and was not excused. In 1745, being the first Visitation after the benefice had been augmented from Queen Anne's Bounty, Stephen Hicks was admonished to obtain a licence. He did not appear at the Visitations of 1749 and 1754. On 28th November 1758, he was licenced as Perpetual Curate upon the nomination of Sir Bourchier Wrey, Bart. At the Visitation held on 1st July 1765, Stephen Hicks is stated to be blind, and his attendance was excused. He appeared, however, at the Visitation of 1768, when he is stated to be infirm and blind, and his attendance at the subsequent Visitations in 1771, 1774, and 1779, was excused.[2]

Stephen Hickes was succeeded by John Basset Collins, Clerk, B.C.L., Rector of Camborne, to which benefice he was instituted in 1771. We have no record of his licence to Temple. He appeared, however, as "Minister" of Temple at the Bishop's Visitations in 1782 and 1786, and dying in June 1790[3] was succeeded at Temple by Bourchier William Wrey, Clerk, M.A., who was licenced to the cure on 13th September 1790, upon the nomination of Sir Bourchier Wrey of Tawstock House, co. Devon, Bart. Upon the death of Bourchier William Wrey, Dalston Clements, Clerk, B.A., Rector of Warleggan, was licenced to the Curacy on the nomination of Sir Bourchier Palk Wrey, and he still holds it, together with the Rectory of Warleggan.

The Chapel, which is dedicated to St. Catherine, is situate in a burial ground containing 2r. 13p., about a furlong south of the ancient road leading through the parish. It has long been in ruins, but the walls still remain sufficiently definite to shew the

---

[1] Original in possession of Mr. Roger Bate of Cardinham.

[2] Stephen Hickes was Rector of Blisland, to which benefice he was instituted in 1718, and died in March 1780, at a very advanced age, after an incumbency of nearly 62 years. He would seem to have held the perpetual curacy of Temple almost as long.

[3] See Hist. of Trigg, Vol. i, p. 329 and Ped. 333.

original plan. (Plate LII, fig. 2.)[1] It consisted of a Chancel 10 ft by 13 ft., nave about
32 ft. by 13 ft., transept or Chapel, 12 ft. by 10 feet, western tower 8 ft. 2 in. by 5 ft. 2 in.
The walls were of good ashlar granite, for which reason the greater part of the base of
the tower with the arch remain in a firm condition, as does also the base of the east
wall of the Chancel. The Chancel would seem to have been lighted by an eastern window,
without splay, probably a late insertion, and two narrow windows much splayed on the
south side; and there was, a doorway, now walled up, in the north wall of the nave.
There was probably a window in the north wall of the Chancel, but the wall having
been thrown down below the position of the window sill, the fact of its existence cannot
be determined with certainty. For the same reason we are unable to state in what
manner the transept, or Chapel, was lighted. There was a small round-headed window in
the tower, the arched head of which, in a single stone, lies on the ground at the foot of
the wall. The tower arch is perfect and rises 11 ft. 6 in. above the floor, and there is
a string-course at the base. The arch rests on imposts, that on the north side having
a plain chamfer underneath, and the other a slight cavetto, apparently of Transition
Norman date. The bowl of an unornamented circular font, of the same period, lies desecrated
within the walls. It is stated that the Chapel bell was twice stolen when the Church fell
into decay, and on the second occasion was irrecoverably lost.[2] The ruins of a building
could be distinguished on the south side of the Chapel yard a quarter of a century since.
In consequence of the absence of visitatorial authority it is said that great irregularities
prevailed. The Curates claimed, and exercised, the right to marry without banns or
licence, hence it became the "Gretna Green" of England. Carew describes it as a place
exempted from the "Bishop's jurisdiction, as once appertayning to the Templers, but not so
from disorders, for if common report communicate with truth, many a bad marriage
bargaine is there yerely slubbred up;" and Tonkin adds: "and grass widows and their
fatlings put to lie in and nurse here."[3] Nevertheless it is remarkable that ecclesiastical
discipline was enforced in this parish as late as in any parish we have noticed.

It is very uncertain at what date divine service ceased to be performed in this
Church. A large ash tree flourishes within its area of more than sixty years growth.
Graves could be distinguished in the churchyard within a recent period, but interments may
have taken place there since divine service has been discontinued in the Church. We
imagine the latter to have been during the latter part of the incumbency of Stephen Hickes,[4]

[1] A description of this Chapel is given by the late Mr. Charles Spence, an antiquary of deserved re-
putation, in his "Iter Cornubiense," read in 1849 before the Exeter Diocesan Architectural Society, and
published in the Transactions of that Society, Vol. iii, p. 220. Mr. Spence would seem, however, to have
become bewildered on the moors, and to have lost his reckoning, for he describes the tower as the Chancel
and mistakes the south side for the north.

[2] Hitchins and Drew, History of Cornwall, vol ii, p. 633. The Rev. C. M. Edward Collins has recently been
using very urgent endeavours to procure the restoration of this ruined Church.

[3] Tonkin's MS. in possession of the Author.

[4] This will agree very nearly with what is stated by Lysons, upon the authority of the late Rev. John
Wallis, Vicar of Bodmin, who says "many aged persons now living (1814) remember the Church standing, and
divine service performed in it." Magna Brit. Vol. iii, p. 303. See also C. S. Gilbert's Hist. of Cornwall,
Vol. ii, p. 621; and Hitchins and Drew's Hist. of Cornwall, Vol. ii, p. 633.

and this conjecture would seem to be confirmed by the fact that the pennance of Edith Galpin in 1777, given in the note below,[1] was ordered to be performed in the Churches of Blisland and Cardinham, no mention being made of her own parish Church.

Donnaton.—Donnaton in the early part of the sixteenth century belonged to John Netherton, and formed a portion of the lands in Temple and St. Breward, which he sold to Thomas Carmynow, Esq., who, by his will dated 16th February 1528, devised the same to Elizabeth his wife to hold to her and her heirs for ever. In 1598, Nicholas Sprey of Bodmin levied a fine of Dorothy Cavel, widow, Francis Courtenay and Phillippa his wife, Richard Courtenay and Oliver Carminow and Mary his wife, which Oliver was grandson of the abovementioned Thomas, in, *inter alia*, Donnnaton and common of pasture.[2] It was afterwards in the family of Kempe. Edward Kempe of Blisland, Gent., by his will dated 8th April 1714, gives to Bridget Kempe his wife, *inter alia*, the tenements of Temple and Donaton in the Parish of Temple. From the Kempe family it passed to George Browne of Bodmin and Trewardale, from whom it has descended to his great-grandson, the Rev. C. N. Edward-Collins of Trewardale, the present possessor.

Abbey Farm.—There is a farm called the " Abbey Farm," which probably was the seat of the Officer of the Commandery.

Merifield.—Merifield in this parish gave its name to an ancient family who possessed it. We find the name frequently mentioned in early records.

Mr. Roger Bate of Cardinham holds lands in this parish which his ancestors have held for several descents. In the reign of Henry VII, these lands belonged to the family of Olyver of Lanke. By charter, dated at Carwen 6th December 18th Henry VII, William Olyver of Lanke, Johanna his wife, and Henry their son, granted to John Olyver and

---

[1] It will perhaps be interesting to our readers to see in what manner sins of incontinency were punished in the Church of England within a century past. Edith Galpin of the Parish of Temple, having been presented at the Archdeacon's Court for having had a base child, and having submitted herself and confessed her crime, was sentenced to perform the pennance following, that is to say, "That you shall on Sunday, the sixth day of April next, in the forenoon, immediately after reading the Second Lesson, enter into the south door of the Parish Church of Blisland; and that on Sunday the thirteenth day of April next, in the forenoon, also immediately after reading the Second Lesson, enter into the south door of the Church of Cardinham, and into each of which said Churches you are to walk bare-footed and bare-legged, your head uncovered and a white sheet hanging down over your shoulders and a white rod in your hand, and shall pass through the middle alley of each of the said Churches so far forth as the Minister's Desk, before which you are to stand until the end of the Nicene Creed. And at the end thereof you are, in each of the said Churches, with an audible voice to say and repeat the words following, to wit: " I Edith Galpin do humbly confess and acknowledge that I have highly offended Almighty God by committing the foul sin of adultery and being thereby as great a scandal to the Church and Christian religion, for which I do hereby declare my hearty sorrow and penitence, and here, in presence of Almighty God and before this congregation promise, by God's assistance, amendment of life for the future, beseeching God to pardon me, and desiring you to pray for me." And thereupon you are with an audible voice, in each of the said Churches, to say and repeat the Lord's Prayer upon your knees. And of your performance hereof you are to bring to the said Court an authentic certificate under the Minister, Churchwardens, and two of the principal inhabitants of each of the said Parishes. Dated 21st March, 1777." To this document are attached the certificates of the Minister and Churchwardens, and certain other inhabitants of the said parishes that she performed the said pennance openly and publicly, according to form and manner prescribed. (Document in the collection of the Author.)

[2] Pedes Finium, 40th Elizabeth, Easter.

Thomas Olyver all their messuages, *inter alia*, in Temple, to secure the payment of forty pence annually to the Wardens of the Store of the Guild of the Blessed Mary of Blyston.[1]

We do not find any Subsidy Roll for Temple until 1641, when the following sums were assessed upon the inhabitants.—[2]

Temple.—								
Marke Penkevell, the Minister of Temple	-		-		-	-	1	0
George Sturtridge	-	-	-	-	-	-	19	6
John Sturtridge	-	-	-	-	~	-	4	0
John Marke, Gent.	-	-	-	-	-	-	3	8
Ralph Sturtridge	-	-	- '	-	-	-	3	0
John Rowe	-	-	-	-	-	-	2	0
Thomas Peperill	-	-	-	-	-	-	1	8
Peter Browne	-	-	-	-	-	-	2	0
William Buckler	-	-	-	-	-	-	1	6
Peter Buckler	-	-	-	-	~	-		11

Sum   -   £1 19 3

We do not find any other detailed assessment, but the sum collected for the Poll Tax in 1666 was 15s.[3] The following table of the assessments for the Hundred for that year will be of interest, as shewing the sums paid, relatively, by each Parish.—

Hundred of } Poll Rate assessed on the several parishes within the said Hundred by
Trigg. } virtue of an Act of Parliament entituled an Act for Raising Moneys by a Poll, and otherwise, towards the maintenance of the present War. (Act 18th and 19th Charles II, Cap 6.)

Breward	-	- 21 9 0	Egloshayle	-	- 37 16 0
Helland	' -	- 9 19 0	St. Minner	-	- 46 13 0
Blisland	-	- 22 4 4	Endellion	-	- 21 13 0
St. Udye	-	- 14 12 4	St. Kew	-	- 49 5 0
St. Mabyn	-	- 27 9 0	St. Teath	-	- 17 18 0
Bodmin Burrough		- 26 7 4	Temple	-	- 15 0
Bodmin Parish	-	- 13 4 8			
					309 5 8

Signed,   WILLIAM THOMS   ◯

EDWARD HOBLYN   ◯

The assessment upon the parish for the year ending 25th March 1672 was £1.[4]

---

[1] Charter penes, Mr. Roger Bate.   [2] Subsidy Roll, 17th Charles $\frac{89}{338}$

[3] Sub. Roll, 18th Charles II. As the tax upon each person was 12d, and there being no resident gentry who would have paid a higher rate, this return will give us the number of the population in 1666 as 15, being the same number as returned in the census of 1801.

[4] Sub. Roll $\frac{89}{358}$

CPSIA information can be obtained
at www.ICGtesting.com
Printed in the USA
BVHW091404141118
533117BV00012B/930/P